BEYOND THE FINISH LINE

BEYOND THE FINISH LINE

THE ART OF
TRANSFORMATIONAL COACHING

DAVID EMEOTT

BEYOND THE FINISH LINE
The Art of Transformational Coaching

Cover Design by Alex Kirkland
Interior Layout and Design by Alice Briggs
Editorial Team: Stephanie Rondeau, Chloie Benton, Teresa Miller

ISBNs:
E-book: 979-8-89165-347-4
Paperback: 979-8-89165-348-1
Hardcover: 979-8-89165-353-5

Published by:
Streamline Books
Kansas City, MO
streamlinebookspublishing.com

Contents

Foreword

N0 ONE WHO knew me at the age of fourteen expected much. I was a troubled, mostly unathletic freshman who struggled in school and couldn't stay out of detention. Just staying out of jail would have been a high enough bar.

Today, I serve as Chief Revenue Officer at a billion-dollar tech company. I've led nonprofit teams in North Africa, written and published a book, and served as a military officer conducting sensitive operations in Afghanistan. I graduated from the Air Force Academy, recognized by the president during his commencement speech, and later earned a master's from MIT. Along the way, I've had the privilege of building a mission-driven company alongside brilliant entrepreneurs.

None of that would have happened had it not been for Coach.

For me, and countless others who have passed through the East Kentwood High School track and field program, Coach Dave Emeott is more than a coach. He was a builder of character, a quiet force of transformation—and, in my own life, the single most influential person in shaping my trajectory.

Working with Coach transformed me. Under his guidance, I went from a lost, undisciplined high schooler to a champion athlete. I learned how to set a goal, build a plan, and show up every day. No excuses. I pushed myself further than I thought possible, and progress followed. Championships followed.

Only later did I realize that winning was never the point. The track was just the medium. What mattered was the process: struggle, failure, commitment, pain, discipline, excellence. On the track, these weren't abstract ideas. They became real, lived experiences that shaped who I was.

By senior year, I had earned a state title and a shot at a top university. As I prepared to board my flight to basic training at the Air Force Academy, with Olympic dreams still in the back of my mind, Coach met me and my family at the airport. He pulled me aside and delivered a message I'll never forget: "This sport has gotten you as far in life as it can. You need to find the thing that will get you to the next place."

It was a terrifying moment. Track had become my identity. But I was beginning to understand: I wasn't just a high school track star anymore. I was becoming something more.

In basic training, I emerged as a leader. The fire, the grit, the relentless drive to be better—they were already inside me.

Over time, those values became instinct. Coach showed me that greatness wasn't a matter of talent, but of mindset. A work ethic. A choice you make every day. It wasn't a single moment of victory but a deeply ingrained pattern in the way you live.

The lessons I learned from Coach—accountability, resilience, preparation, humility, team before self—have echoed through every chapter of my life. Whether in the classroom, volunteering overseas, leading teams in combat, building a business, or showing up as a husband and father, they've shaped how I lead and how I live. Not as motivational quotes, but as muscle memory.

Whether you're a coach, a parent, a military officer, or a business leader, the principles here matter. This book is not about winning races. It's a blueprint for guiding people to realize the potential within themselves—as athletes, as professionals, and as people.

It's an honor to offer this foreword as a small tribute to the man who shaped my life and the lives of so many others.

On behalf of all of us—thank you, Coach.
Erik Mirandette

Introduction

Building a Championship Culture

From 2007 to 2019, East Kentwood High School track and field dominated the sport in the state of Michigan and competed regularly on the national stage, including winning a national championship in 2010. In that thirteen-year stretch, we earned eight state titles and three runner-up finishes, an accomplishment any program would be proud of.

But this book isn't about winning.

It's about why we won and how transformational coaching shaped our athletes, our team culture, and the people they became beyond the track.

This book is about character, perseverance, and the lessons I've learned along the way. It's not just a story of victories but one of transformation and purpose. It is my hope that coaches will see this book as a window into a program that experienced both success and struggles. Coaching is hard—it often comes with little reward or praise and, for most high school coaches, even less money.

I hope every coach prioritizes the development of their athletes as people first. Transformational coaching will win in the long run, both on and off the field. Conversely, transactional coaching may lead to short-term success, but it rarely leaves a lasting impact on a student's life.

Transformational Coaching

My coaching journey began with high hopes and dreams of where my teams would end up and what they could accomplish. In hindsight, we were trying to win things back then we had no business believing we could win. But decades later, after all the trophies and championships, the thing I am most proud of is that our program became transformational for hundreds of young adults.

At the time, we didn't know the terminology—the differences between "transactional" and "transformational" coaching—but we did know that we wanted to change lives and use athletics as the vehicle to do it. This book will take you on a journey through the highs and lows of athletics during our pursuit. Looking back, there were times when we were transactional, which brought short-term success, and times when we were transformational, where we may have failed in the short term but won in the long run.

Transformational does not mean being weak or soft. In fact, it is often quite the opposite. Being transformational means putting the athlete first in every situation, prioritizing their future above all else. Many times, coaches are faced with the opportunity of letting poor behavior slide for the sake of winning. Choosing this option is transactional, as if asking the athlete, "What can you do for me today?"

Transformational coaching, on the other hand, asks, "How will my decision impact you as a person long term?"

In this book, we will explore that journey. Wins and losses come and go, but the character our former athletes have displayed is truly what defines success.

First-Time Head Coach

In 2001, I was named the head cross-country coach at East Kentwood High School, also known as "EK," and, in 2004, I became the head track and field coach. In those roles, I fully believed we could do things that had rarely been accomplished in West Michigan. At that time, only two West Michigan teams had ever won a Division 1 state title: Traverse City Central, coached by the legendary John Lober, and Portage Northern, led by Bill Fries, an amazing coach and mentor to me. I've often reflected on what was different prior to West Michigan teams starting to compete with the best in the state. Were our goals too small back then? Did we fail to push one another enough? If "iron sharpens iron," maybe the west side of the state simply didn't have enough iron to go around in those days.

Now, things are different: West Michigan teams are consistently competitive with programs from the greater Detroit area. But when I started, winning a conference or regional title was a major accomplishment—and winning a state championship in track and field nearly unheard of.

To reach that level, I knew we'd need to work hard, but sustaining greatness over time would require more than talent. It would take a consistent plan focused on character education, a high-quality staff of coaches, and, overall, a fully transformational approach.

Building Character

If true greatness means more than just winning track meets, then we had to focus on what truly mattered: growing great people within our program. That meant building character and holding athletes accountable for all of their actions, on and off the track. Toward this end, I began designing daily character lessons. We met for practice every day at 2:45, beginning with a character lesson, many of which you'll find in this book. These lessons covered everything: how to shake hands, meet people, treat officials, respect elders, and more.

Each talk was tailored to the needs of our students. If an issue arose, we'd adjust the lessons to accommodate it. For example, if a team member had stolen something, we'd discuss integrity under the following assumption: "If you lie, you cheat. If you cheat, you steal." I'd ask my team, "Why don't most sixty-five-year-olds steal from each other?" The obvious answer would be that, by the time you are sixty-five, you have matured and realized all of your actions have consequences not only for yourself but for others.

These discussions created thought-provoking moments. For sixteen-year-olds, it was a chance to sit quietly and focus, free from distractions like cell phones. I often reiterated: "This is a character lesson. They say losing builds character, but we have no plans to lose, so we need to take this time to learn."

East Kentwood High School: A Place Like No Other

East Kentwood High School, the home of the Falcons, stands as one of the most vibrant and diverse communities in the country. We are proudly recognized as the most diverse high school in Michigan and consistently rank among the top ten most diverse schools in the United States.

When I talk about diversity, I mean it in every sense of the word—racial, cultural, linguistic, religious, and socioeconomic. On any given day, over eighty languages are spoken in our hallways. We serve nearly three thousand students in grades 9 through 12, making us the largest high school in Michigan. Our student population reflects an extraordinary cross section of the world. We have students who drive BMWs to school and others whose families do not own a car. Roughly 74 percent of our students come from minority backgrounds, and over 55 percent qualify for free or reduced-price lunch, indicating significant economic need.

These challenges are real. Many of our students face daily stressors related to poverty, food insecurity, or unstable housing. As a result, school often becomes more than just a place to learn—it becomes a place of safety, structure, and hope. Teachers and coaches at EK frequently serve not only as educators but also as mentors, role models, and even parental figures.

Despite these barriers, EK is defined not by hardship but by resilience and opportunity. Our staff, families, and community partners work tirelessly to support student success, both academically and personally. While we continue to address achievement gaps—especially in areas like math—we do so with the unwavering belief that all students can thrive when they are seen, supported, and held to high expectations.

East Kentwood isn't just a high school. It's a global community under one roof, and it's a place where greatness is pursued daily by students and staff alike.

In 2007, East Kentwood placed second at the Michigan High School Athletic Association (MHSAA) state meet, the highest finish in school history. We were runners-up again in 2008. Finally, in 2009, we won the state title.

In 2010, our team of 125 boys won the MHSAA state title, the New Balance Nationals title, and was ranked the number one team in the nation by Nike. By the time the pandemic hit in 2020, East Kentwood had won eight state titles, achieved three runner-up finishes, and set multiple all-time state records. We've had the privilege of sending many student-athletes to colleges all across the country. But what I'm most proud of is this: We achieved a 100 percent high school graduation rate for our track and field athletes—and nearly every one of them left with a clear postgraduation plan, whether it was college, military service, trade school, or the workforce.

It was our mission to ensure that no student left our program without a direction toward the next chapter of their life.

At times, we were criticized for encouraging some students to pursue college even when others believed they weren't quite ready. We accept that criticism, but we also know the full story: Many of those same young people started at a local community college, gained confidence, and a few years later were working in careers they never imagined possible.

Yes, some struggled. Some found the academic demands too high or realized they weren't mature enough for the full college experience. But even in those cases, I know this: They had an opportunity, one that many in their families never had. And even if they didn't finish college, they began shaping a new narrative of academic achievement for their families.

I can't count how many times former athletes have brought their own children back to me and proudly said, "Coach, look how smart they are—not like me." It may be a bittersweet statement as well as a point of pride for them, but either way, I do know this: We're moving the ball forward one generation at a time.

BEYOND THE FINISH LINE

CHAPTER 1

My Story

August 5, 1992: Saginaw County Courtroom

I was seventeen years old, freshly graduated from high school and just weeks away from starting college. Instead of preparing for a dorm room or picking classes, I was sitting in a courtroom waiting to learn my sentence.

My mom sat behind me, silent but anxious. I was seated next to a court-appointed attorney I had just met, facing the Honorable Judge Patrick Meter, who was about to decide my future. My crimes had been committed nearly a year earlier, and I had confessed to every one of them—no legal strategy, no negotiations, just the truth.

The sentence came swiftly: thirty days in jail and two months of house arrest.

This wasn't juvenile detention; this was real jail. No special wings for kids. I was processed immediately and placed into a cell with seven grown men, most of them much older, many awaiting trial.

Among them was a man accused of murder and another accused of molesting a child.

That night, I laid in my bunk, terrified. I cried.

I didn't know what came next, but I knew I had time to think.

The Beginning

Some people are born with success handed to them from the start, while others seem to have everything stacked against them from day one. It might be easy to assume that one type of person will succeed while the other will fail. However, it's not always that simple. And as you'll read in the pages of this book, the variables that lead to success often have nothing to do with where you came from. Rather, they have everything to do with how you choose to move forward and which leaders you find to influence you along the way.

I was born to a single mother and never met my real father. I know she did everything she could to keep me safe. As tough as my life was, hers was just as hard, and we went through those difficult times together.

From birth to age five, we lived in various low-income housing situations, from trailers to apartments. When I was six, my mother met my stepfather, an alcoholic foundry worker for General Motors. Because of him, I spent more than a few nights in halfway houses for battered women and children. Despite multiple breakups, however, my mother never left him. Over time, I gained two younger brothers, Matt and Joe, and we continued bouncing from home to home, attending different elementary schools.

My brothers and I have always loved each other deeply, but life was hard. That hardship taught us resilience, empathy, and a genuine appreciation for the things others might take for granted. Even as I grew older and was able to stay in one school for longer periods, I struggled to fit in. The summer after my ninth grade year, I received a letter at home from the high school track and cross-country coach, Doug Frank. He had written to tell me I did a great job on the mile run in gym class. It was a handwritten letter, and little did I know, he probably wrote a hundred of these every summer. But at that moment, it didn't matter—I had never had anyone see me as an athlete before, and receiving that letter became a pivotal moment in my life.

Coach Frank was the most straightforward and honest person I knew. He was very frank—pun intended. He wasn't always the nicest or most friendly coach, but he pulled no punches and told you exactly how it was. I wouldn't say I was particularly close with Coach Frank, but I do believe he cared about me. He pushed me hard and expected nothing but my best effort. The time I spent with him made me a completely different person than I was in the other twenty-two hours of my day. I wanted to do my best for him.

Coach Frank was also a math teacher and a graduate of Central Michigan University. On many occasions, he sat me down and explained how my poor decisions would affect my future. I distinctly remember one time when he asked me if I enjoyed my life. He knew full well that my life outside of school and sports was pretty rough.

"Do you want to provide this life for your kids?" he asked.

"God gave you the ability to learn," he continued. "You have been given the gift of being a very good math student, but you waste your time in class. You are destined to live in that same trailer park and give your kids the same life." These comments did not feel great at the time, but somehow they were just what I needed.

I've had an interesting relationship with Coach Frank over the years. I always felt like I wanted to be his star pupil, but the reality was probably much simpler—I was just another kid in the program, another young athlete that Coach Frank poured his time and effort into. And like so many others before me, I am forever grateful that he did.

The Downward Spiral

The summer between my junior and senior years, my life took a turn for the worse. To avoid going home, I often stayed at various friends' and acquaintances' houses. Unfortunately, some of the couches I slept on belonged to friends who weren't always making the wisest choices. Looking back, I know now that a sixteen-year-old version of me was not equipped to make my own decisions.

I started running with a group that was breaking into a sporting goods store selling mostly baseball and soccer equipment. Although I wasn't a baseball player and certainly not a soccer player, I went along a few times before realizing it wasn't worth the risk.

By my senior year, I appeared to be on a better course. I was on the cross-country, golf, hockey, and track teams—all while working part-time at the local gas station. Staying active gave me an escape from my home life.

But I was living a double life.

During the day, I worked hard at practice and tried to represent myself well. I was even the president of the student council. At night, I ran the streets and entertained any wild idea my friends and I could come up with. I thought I was smarter than my coaches and teachers, but my life wasn't improving.

That winter, in need of a coat, I walked into a department store without a coat on and picked out a nice winter jacket and walked out the door. Emboldened, I did it again for a cousin who needed one. Although I got away with it, eventually, the group breaking into the sports store got caught. During their arrest, they implicated everyone involved—including me.

When I was arrested, I didn't have an attorney. I spilled my guts about every crime I had committed without legal representation. So much for "You have the right to remain silent"—I did not exercise that right. The charges? Breaking and entering and theft. And, to top it off, I confessed to stealing the winter coats. Because one coat was valued at over $100, that charge alone carried serious implications.

Many of my codefendants had lawyers. They navigated the system and came out with misdemeanors, no jail time, and clean records. But I had committed three unrelated felonies. My sentencing would not be so kind. As mentioned in the introduction, on August 5, 1992, I lived my own version of *Scared Straight*. I was sentenced to thirty days in Saginaw County Jail and two months of house arrest. At seventeen years old, I was locked up with the child molester, the man charged with murder, and a group of others in for petty theft and DUIs. For many nights after that first one, I cried in my bunk, terrified, wondering what I had done to myself.

I had officially hit rock bottom. I wasn't thinking about the future. I wasn't setting goals. I just knew I had to be better. I had to change. New friends. New attitude. New life.

Days in jail were cold and sterile. I passed the time playing cards and listening to the other cellmates' stories. Over time, I realized most of these guys weren't monsters. They were people who had made bad decisions.

One inmate—awaiting trial for murder—became the leader of our group. He had kids, one about my age. And as strange as it sounds, he had a good heart. He talked to me about life, and a common theme in those conversations was this: *It's not too late for you.*

For him and the others, their paths were pretty much set. But I was still young. Even though the law saw me as an adult, I was just a seventeen-year-old kid with a chance to start over. Looking back, I was a good kid. I cared about people, had a lot of friends, and my heart was never filled with hate or anger—even though I probably had every reason to feel that way. Like most sixteen- or seventeen-year-olds, I made a lot of bad choices. But a few of mine led to a life-altering experience—an experience that would completely change the trajectory of my life.

At the time, I couldn't have known how valuable that moment would become. It gave me perspective, purpose, and a deep understanding that I now carry with me every day. What once felt like failure turned out to be one of the most important turning points in my life.

Every night in that cell, I prayed the same prayer:

No more lying. No more cheating. No more stealing. Lord, help me be better.

I knew I had to change. Real change may not typically happen overnight—but at seventeen, I grew up more than I ever had before.

That fall, I enrolled at Saginaw Valley State University and joined the track team. To be honest, I had no business going to college; I wasn't ready academically, emotionally, or socially. But the idea of being part of a team again pulled me in.

I began fall conditioning while still under house arrest, only allowed to leave for school and work. Back in the early nineties, house arrest meant wearing a giant black ankle monitor, not a discreet device. Hiding it during practice was impossible. It was awkward. It was embarrassing.

But was it enough to stop me? No.

And in the aftermath of my time served, when I determined to make changes and keep going, my second chance truly began.

Climbing Back Up

I had a promising first year in track and field, but my grades were terrible. I was on the verge of being dismissed from school. I had cheated my way through high school, and without that crutch of academic deception, college hit me hard. I didn't know how to study, and I didn't know how to ask for help. What's more, I had no backup plan.

In the summer of 1993, I got a job as a lifeguard at Haithco Lake in Saginaw. A year after my time in jail, I was still a work in progress, trying to figure out who I was going to become. And then, during a short fifteen-minute lifeguard break, a coworker introduced me to a friend of hers.

Her name was Heather.

To this day, I can still remember what that moment felt like. It was like something out of a movie. I was immediately in love, and I knew without a doubt that she was the one I wanted to spend the rest of my life with.

On July 3, 1993, I went on my first date with Heather, and everything changed. I doubt whether she was as immediately sold on me. In fact, I knew she wasn't. It took a while to convince her that I was a different person than the one who had gone to jail. I had already changed quite a bit, but in the process of trying to win her over, I changed even more. And if you know Heather, you know I had a lot of work to do to reassure her trust in me.

She was dating a boy who had a long way to go. I wasn't proud of where I'd been, and I wasn't yet confident in where I was going. If I'm being completely honest, I still don't know exactly why she chose me. But she did, and in many ways, she saved my life. For the first time, I had a reason to live for something beyond myself.

That fall, Heather was attending Central Michigan University, and I was in my second year at SVSU. I'd visit her at her apartment, which was always buzzing with roommates and their boyfriends. It was a lively social hangout. But one night, in the middle of the week, while I was trying to convince everyone to go out to the local bar, Heather pulled me aside and asked me to meet her in her room.

I'll never forget the look in her eyes: disappointment, frustration— and something deeper. This was not a playful conversation; this was serious. We had never even had an argument up to that point, but this felt like a line-in-the-sand moment.

She asked me if I was okay and then said, "We all have tests and studying to do—I thought you did too. Your grades are terrible, and you're doing nothing to change that."

There were more words exchanged—stern ones—and while I can't recall them exactly, I remember how they made me feel. Heather thought she was dating someone smart. Someone with drive who was serious about building a future. But I wasn't holding up my end. She wasn't going to settle for mediocrity—and she made that crystal clear.

At that moment, something shifted. I had always believed that there were plenty of smart people who struggled in school. But to Heather, grades weren't just about being naturally gifted—they were about effort, discipline, and integrity. If I wanted to be someone she could be proud of, I had to work hard to change. Right then, her belief became mine.

And if school was just a game requiring a strategy, then I could figure out how to win it. I was always good at games. I just hadn't cared about that one—until now. With Heather's encouragement, my priorities completely transformed.

I became a decent pole vaulter, scoring a point at the Great Lakes Intercollegiate Athletic Conference championships. More importantly, I became a dedicated student. I started studying more intently, turning in assignments early. I sat in the front row and asked questions. By the end of my sophomore year, I earned straight A's.

The following year, I gave up competing as a pole vaulter for Saginaw Valley State University and transferred to Central Michigan University. I was certainly in need of a change in scenery and the opportunity to get yet some more separation from my old life and continue my journey to a new life. I went on to earn a degree in secondary education, majoring in mathematics. I became the first person in my extended family to graduate from college.

After that, things happened quickly. I followed in Doug Frank's footsteps and became a straight-shooting math teacher and coach with a mission to transform lives through athletics. Upon graduation from CMU, I landed a teaching job at East Kentwood High School. And over the years as a math teacher, I enjoyed success: I was nominated more than once for Michigan Teacher of the Year, becoming a finalist in 2014. I can't imagine Coach Frank or any of my K–12 teachers would have thought that was possible.

My story is one of an immature kid with a rough upbringing who, in this amazing country, was given a second chance. For that, I am thankful every single day. I've worked constantly to fulfill the promise I made that lonely night in jail: to be the best version of myself possible. Part of that promise became a determination to give back to the kids I'm so blessed to coach. While my criminal record has been erased, I am still blessed to have had those negative experiences that, in a strange way, changed my life for the better.

CHAPTER 2

Choose Transformational Coaches

*A coach will impact more young people in a year
than the average person does in a lifetime.*
—Billy Graham

ICK SABAN, ARGUABLY the greatest coach of all time, famously discussed the concept of transactional versus transformational coaching during his time at Michigan State University, and his words resonate with me deeply. Saban pinpointed a specific moment in his career—his tenth game at MSU in 1998—as the turning point when he realized he needed to be a transformational coach. This shift in philosophy would serve him and his future teams enormously well, particularly at Alabama, where he led the Crimson Tide to multiple national championships between 2007 and 2023.

As an MSU fan, I remember Saban's time there in the nineties. He was not yet the coach who would later dominate at Alabama, but he found a powerful approach to coaching during that time. As he explains, transformational coaching is about developing athletes as people. It's about coaching with a focus on growth, helping athletes succeed and learn from failure. The opposite of this is transactional coaching, which is purely outcome-based. If a team wins, the coach rewards them; if they lose, the coach tears them down. The athlete's value is tied only to what they can do for the coach in that moment.

I have spent my career striving to be a transformational leader, shaping young men and women into strong, capable adults in life—not just successful competitors on the track. Every day, we push athletes to their limits while ensuring they know they are unconditionally valued. Given my successes with this approach, I would encourage every parent to prioritize finding transformational coaches. In fact, I'd go as far as to say that young athletes should choose a coach over a sport.

It is my hope that every high school athlete has the opportunity to work with a transformational, long-term mentor. I loved my days as a teacher, and I worked hard to make an impact. From time to time, I did. But in the classroom, I only had one hour a day with students for a semester—maybe an entire year if I was lucky. By comparison, I spend years coaching athletes. We've traveled across the country together, enduring long bus rides, high-pressure meets, and moments of pure joy as well as crushing defeat. This long-term mentorship has allowed me to go beyond merely coaching a sport, and toward being a mentor for life.

As an athletic director, I am constantly searching for transformational coaches. I often start by looking at the teachers in our school building who already demonstrate transformational leadership daily. I can teach someone the X's and O's of a sport, but natural leadership is what our athletes truly need, and I prioritize this attribute over expertise in any sport.

Transformational leaders aren't limited to teachers and coaches. Think about the incredible mentors who can be found within a school: the band instructor who inspires their students, the student council director who instills confidence, or even the lunch lady who serves meals with a smile every day for years. Transformational figures are everywhere. I often think about the potential impact of a first boss—someone who can either build confidence or tear it down—and how critical that person can be for someone first entering the workforce.

Conversely, most people can remember an adult in their life who was merely transactional, someone who only valued them when they performed well. As soon as they no longer served a purpose, they were often cast aside by transactional leaders.

One of the best presentations I've ever seen on this topic came from my friend and colleague, Rich Fulford, the school head at the Christian Academy of Knoxville. Rich, a former elite pole vaulter at the University of Tennessee, credits his coaching philosophy to his college coach, Jim Bemiller. When I saw Rich at the National Pole Vault Summit in Reno, Nevada, Rich used the movie *The Karate Kid* as a model for transformational and transactional coaching.

Mr. Miyagi represents the ultimate transformational coach: He deeply cares about Daniel's growth as a person. Meanwhile, John Kreese, the Cobra Kai coach, is the definition of transactional coaching, focused solely on winning at all costs, in particular cynically exploiting his star student, Johnny Lawrence. While these characters are extreme examples, the lesson is clear.

What parent would willingly choose John Kreese to mentor their child? Yes, Johnny did become one of the top karate students in the valley under Kreese's philosophy, but at what cost? In reality, most coaches exist somewhere between these two extremes. We'd all like to be Mr. Miyagi, but there's a constant struggle between being transformational while still achieving competitive success. (After all, asking a football team to wash cars every day for practice—"wax on, wax off"—might not be the best recipe for championships.)

Overall, I encourage parents to evaluate the morals and character of the coaches they choose for their children. These mentors will spend more time with your kids during high school than almost anyone else. When our own children played different sports, my wife and I prioritized finding coaches of high character, even if they weren't the most knowledgeable. We've had plenty of moments watching youth sports when we cringed at how coaches handled their teams, often screaming at officials or humiliating players. We knew we didn't want that for our own kids.

I don't remember the record of a single sub-varsity team my kids played on, but I do remember the lessons they learned, the fun they had, and the relationships they built. The quality of experience is always more important than wins and losses.

As an athletic director, evaluating these qualities in coaches is one of the hardest parts of the job. Transformational coaches don't always look like saints, and transactional coaches don't always look like villains. Sometimes, the truest picture emerges by listening to the athletes. When kids speak passionately about how much they love playing for their coach and how that coach pushes them to succeed on the field and in the classroom, I know we've got something special.

When I was a young pole vault coach, I was given the mission of coaching girls for the first time. Up to that point in my career, I had only coached boys for three full seasons. I was young, confident, and convinced I knew everything. With this fourth season of coaching, it didn't take long for me to realize how little I actually knew.

To be honest, I wasn't exactly thrilled with the assignment. On day one, I walked in and gave them my best John Kreese impression from *The Karate Kid*, barking orders.

"There will be no crying, no whining, no hugs, and you will work just as hard as the boys," I told them. The girls bought in, and I was excited to coach them.

A few weeks later, we had our first relay-style pole vault competition. I hyped it up, telling them I had *never* lost a relay in my four years of coaching and wasn't about to start now. The girls were motivated by my determination. They wanted to win.

Unfortunately, I hadn't done my homework on the opposition. We lost to a pair of twin pole vaulters who had been training for years and already had college scholarships lined up. My girls were crushed by the defeat, and they cried. True to my "no crying" rule, I reminded them of our agreement. One of the girls, Kate, looked at me with teary eyes and said, "I know we agreed not to cry, but it seemed so important to you."

My heart sank. I realized, in that moment, that I had been acting like an idiot. These girls weren't crying because they were weak. They were crying because they cared about *me*. Unfortunately, I had made it all about me and not about them. From that day forward, the rules changed: Cry when you need to, support your teammates, and never hesitate to give hugs.

Coaching those girls transformed me as much as—I hope—I transformed them.

Athlete Profile: Macey Emeott, Class of 2022

Macey is our second child, and she transformed me into a proud girl dad. Growing up in a dysfunctional household with three boys, I had no idea how much having a daughter would change me. From the day she was born, Macey has been the kindest, gentlest person I've ever known. She has taught me that not everything has to be black and white, that not all problems have immediate solutions, and that sometimes we just need to sit with sadness to move past it.

I often say I was born into a cold, dark, and mean place. I've spent my whole life trying to emerge from this and become a kinder person, and without Macey, I'm not sure I ever would have gotten there. She has taught me more than I can ever express.

In our community, volleyball has always been a standout sport for EK, with their program winning multiple state titles and helping grow strong young women. We knew early on that getting Macey involved in this program would be amazing for her. Prior to her first year in high school, we were excited to get Macey involved with our local club, Far Out Volleyball, led by transformational coaches Joe and Roxanne Steenhuysen. Competing in this highly competitive environment helped Macey develop an edge while maintaining her natural compassion, understanding that people always come first.

Like any parent, I wanted to raise my kids in an environment free of hardship, especially my little girl. For all the struggles I endured growing up, I wanted to protect her from experiencing anything similar. I wished for a smooth, carefree life for her, one filled with princesses and rainbows. But the reality is, life is hard, and I won't always be there to shield her. Our goal was to prepare the child for the road, not the road for the child.

Athletics, especially volleyball, became an excellent tool for building resilience. The wins and losses were real and wholly felt. There were times Macey failed, and times she succeeded. On more than one occasion, she found herself at the service line for match point. Sometimes, she hit the ball square into the net, and her team lost. Other times, she served an ace, and they won. The difference of just a few feet could completely swing her emotions from joy to devastation. But through it all, athletics provided a safe space to experience real failure and learn from it.

Today, Macey is a tough, independent kid. I have no doubt that great things are in her future, but I also know she will face challenges along the way. The difference is, she is equipped to handle both through her time as a young athlete.

Raising a teenage girl has been full of ups and downs, but I've learned more lessons from Macey than I can count. She's taught me to listen more and try to solve problems less. I've learned not to take her side too quickly when she says she hates her former best friend, because teenage girls have a way of making up even after seemingly final declarations. And then suddenly, I'm the one left explaining why I don't like her friend anymore while she's moved on. Most importantly, I've learned that sometimes all she needs is a hug, some ice cream, and the knowledge that I'm proud of her. Macey went on to compete as a pole vaulter for Saginaw Valley State University and is working on a degree in Kinesiology.

Macey competing in the pole vault in high school

CHAPTER 3

Patience: They Grow Up Between Fourteen and Forty

It does not matter how slowly you go as long as you do not stop.
—Confucius

AS AN EDUCATOR who has spent most of my life working with high school students, there is one undeniable truth I've come to know: We are privileged to witness the most impressionable and developmental stage in a young adult's life. Watching young men and women grow—not just physically but mentally and emotionally—is one of the greatest honors in education and coaching.

It's a saying we use often: "We all grow up between fourteen and forty. The closer you get to fourteen, the better your life will be. The closer to forty, the more you'll struggle." This concept drives many of the conversations I have with students and athletes. I think of myself as that young, immature kid sitting in a jail cell—closer to fourteen than forty in every way that mattered. But in that moment, I had to grow up fast.

Think about yourself in fifth grade. Think about the athletes you admired, the video games you loved, and the music you listened to. How much has changed? As much as a child grows from fifth to eighth grade, they will grow even more from ninth to twelfth. Growth, in all its forms, is inevitable, but what's important is learning how to grow not only from success, but from failure as well. We either win, or we learn. During this time as teenagers, we experience a lot of learning. It is important that we have the right mentors around us.

Teaching athletes and students to fail forward is a life skill that will benefit them in all aspects of their journey. Failure can be an accelerator for success if channeled correctly. Everyone can earn an A in school—no one earns their grade at the expense of another student. Athletics, however, has winners and losers. Failing in athletics is just a part of the process. In fact, losing is a critical aspect of athletics. No one would be interested in a sport where one team always wins. I guess the exception is the Harlem Globetrotters, who have famously beaten the Washington Generals for over fifty years. But in real sports, losing is a reality of the process.

I often set a schedule that guarantees our team will face tough competition and experience losses. We purposely schedule teams and meets where we can be challenged—where our athletes can experience defeat, even if it's just a single loss. I often say that the goal of sports is to travel no further than necessary to get beaten at least once. If I can lose in my hometown, why would I travel three hundred miles away for the same lesson?

But the opposite is also true. Staying in your backyard to protect a winning streak stifles real growth. The sadness that comes from a loss is one of the most motivating things an athlete will ever feel. If, after losing, you aren't motivated to get to work, you might simply be in the wrong sport.

I am always impressed by great athletes who hit the gym the day after a world championship loss. I often think, for example, about

Michael Jordan in the weight room after those losses to my Detroit Pistons in the late eighties.

You could see him developing strength in spite of those losses—and it was just a matter of time. In the end, being defeated by Detroit played a huge role in Jordan becoming the greatest of all time. During my childhood, MJ famously lost to the Pistons year after year in the Eastern Conference finals, the last step before the championship. What if Michael Jordan had never lost all of those Eastern Conference games? Would he be as great? Certainly not.

How will you, as a transformational coach, use losses to help your team and your athletes grow?

High school students will see physical changes in their bodies simply because biology takes its course. Mental and emotional maturity, however, are not guaranteed. It depends on the presence of strong influencers—coaches, teachers, mentors—who challenge young people to question their decisions and see beyond the immediate. Great mentors understand that kids will make mistakes. But beyond success and failure, the real question is "Can you see them for who they have the potential to become, rather than judging them only by the choices they're making today?" Because, so often, those mistakes are just the result of immaturity, not an actual lack of potential.

Long-term mentorship is one of the most important factors in a young adult's growth. Again, as a teacher, I could impact my students one hour a day, five days a week, for a semester or, at most, a year. While I made some really great connections in that time, these did not compare to the ones I made during the course of an athlete's four-year career. Coaches hold the unique power to help young people develop into thoughtful, responsible adults, and it became my mission in life to impact young people in a permanently positive way. I know I was placed here for a reason, and I believe that if I give them what they need, I can help make their lives better.

I've seen countless examples of students who entered high school with a bad reputation—kids others labeled as "troublemakers" or "lost causes." But growth is possible for everyone. With patience and guidance, these kids often become unrecognizable versions of their former selves by senior year.

As parents, mentors, or coaches, we often want to accelerate our children's growth and maturity, but the reality is that we cannot be cocoon cutters. To become a butterfly takes time, requiring patience from everyone involved. This is most often the case for teams that lack upperclassmen or must rely on young stars to play critical roles. Younger athletes have not been through the battles the way upperclassmen have. They are seeing things for the first time and have not had the experience to reflect on how different situations should be handled. As coaches, we want sophomores to perform like seniors, with poise, precision, and consistency, but maturation takes time, and growth can't be rushed, only guided. Pushing the process can lead to disastrous results.

A rebuilding year in athletics is a season when everyone involved understands that the primary goal is not immediate success, but long-term growth. It's a time to step back, recalibrate the team's goals, and focus on what can be accomplished now to lay the foundation for future success.

The concept of a rebuilding year is real and must be handled with intention. It can be a critical period in a program's journey. Often, we see teams that operate in cycles—every few years, they become competitive again. That success doesn't happen by accident. It comes from the time they invested in development, unity, and growth during those rebuilding seasons.

Our goal as transformational coaches must be to approach every class the same way, developing each group with the same level of care and patience. Giving underclassmen some cover from older, stronger athletes while they develop is crucial. Even if a younger athlete has the ability to compete at the state level, expectations should be managed carefully.

Cutting corners on this deliberate process often leads to overwhelming expectations, which are frequently followed by injuries and mental setbacks.

Athlete Profile: Erik Mirandette, Class of 2000

Erik was the kind of kid some people might have called a "throwaway." His parents went through a difficult divorce when he was young, and even by the time he was in elementary school, a principal had said he would "end up in jail someday." Comments like this struck close to home for me.

His parents' divorce was ugly and hard on the kids. Erik and his younger brother spent equal time between their mother's home and their father's. Erik's father, a karate instructor, had very high expectations for his sons and enforced strict policies to keep them in line. These high expectations, combined with rigid rules, pushed Erik to become fiercely independent. As a result, Erik was an angry young man without many positive outlets for his energy. He made life challenging for his teachers and principals, often displaying behavior that could be labeled euphemistically as "attention-seeking." However, the reality was that Erik simply chose to do things the hard way, making it far more difficult for himself. This reminded me of myself at that age.

Erik was an incredible fighter—he wanted to challenge and fight everyone and everything. This fighting spirit was in him from a young age, but he didn't know how to channel it positively. Most of his teachers did not see this aggression as a positive, but I knew if I could channel this energy in the right way, we could find greatness.

When Erik joined the track team his freshman year, I was a twenty-two-year-old math teacher in my first year of coaching at EK. Even so, I knew I could help him. And deep down, whether he realized it or not, I knew Erik was at an inflection point. Early on, we sat down and talked about his goals. It didn't take long to realize he didn't have a plan—but he did have passion. My job was clear: Help him turn that passion into a purpose by giving him a plan with a path forward.

We started more as brothers than as coach and athlete. We were only a few years apart and it was easy to play the big brother role. Over time, I watched Erik mature and grow stronger, both physically and mentally. I had a front-row seat as he learned to channel his energy into something powerful and positive.

By his junior year, Erik had developed into the top pole vaulter in the state of Michigan and one of the best in the entire Midwest. His grit helped him overcome potentially devastating setbacks. At the state championships that year, he rolled his ankle during warm-ups. It was a crushing moment, but just another obstacle for Erik to overcome. And he did. That day, despite the injury, Erik rose to the occasion and won a state title.

His journey from a troubled kid with no plan to a state champion drew the attention of top universities, including Florida, Michigan, and the United States Air Force Academy. He had become the kind of coveted student-athlete few people believed he could be.

As someone who knew Erik well, I assumed he would choose one of the major universities where he could flourish as both an athlete and a person. I was shocked when he visited my classroom to discuss his decision and told me he had chosen the Air Force Academy. I couldn't understand why he would pick a military academy over a school like Florida, where he could enjoy the life of a college track athlete. Instead, he was choosing to become a soldier, start his college experience in boot camp, and endure the rigors of military training for the next four years. He declined the conventional golden ticket and accepted admission to a more unique and difficult program.

When queried about his choice, his response was simple: "That's where special people go and special things happen."

Almost unwittingly, Erik became the ultimate leader, undergoing an incredible transformation throughout our time together. He didn't realize that he wasn't just transforming himself—he was inspiring those around him. Over the next five years, three more athletes from East Kentwood High School chose the Air Force Academy. Two were pole vaulters, and one joined the academy's triathlon team. All four graduated and fulfilled their commitment to the U.S. Air Force, going on to do special things. And it was all thanks to Erik's leadership.

As a member of the Air Force, Erik's incredible fighting spirit became a priceless military asset. At the academy, he was a natural leader admired by both professors and generals. He thrived in an environment where high expectations were paired with strict discipline, which allowed his natural leadership abilities to shine. After graduating, Erik was selected to a highly competitive special military unit and led offensive counterintelligence operations and clandestine intelligence collections missions throughout the Middle East and other parts of the world. As a leader of soldiers, Erik combined his natural charisma with his relentless drive to fight for what was right, keeping us all safe.

But with a promising military career ahead and on a fast track for promotion, Erik once again chose the road less traveled. He decided to give it all up and go back to school to pursue an MBA. He walked away from a successful career in the armed forces, where he had power, rank, and influence, to pursue a new challenge. Many questioned why he would make such a dramatic change, but Erik saw an opportunity for growth. He earned acceptance into an elite MBA program at MIT and was awarded the Pat Tillman Scholarship for his dedication and service.

Today, Erik is forty years old and married with two kids. He holds a C-level position at a major company in Boston, Massachusetts. I am so proud of this young man for all the growth he has achieved. Erik's story is a testament to the power of transformation, leadership, high expectations, and the courage to choose unfamiliar, challenging paths with potentially great rewards.

CHAPTER 4

Relationships: The Real Steroid

People don't care how much you know until
they know how much you care.
—John C. Maxwell

HERE'S A SAYING that has guided my coaching philosophy for years: "Men bond at war, women bond to go to war." It's a reminder that men and women connect with each other differently, and as a coach, you can't treat them the same if you want to succeed.

Coaching both genders simultaneously has taught me to adapt my approach. My methods for the boys' team wouldn't work as effectively for the girls', and vice versa. For example, with female athletes, I emphasize team bonding early in the season. Building strong connections before adversity strikes is crucial. Team outings, like a preseason rowing clinic our volleyball team attended last year, create trust and camaraderie that pay dividends later.

For boys, the bonding often happens naturally through shared experiences, especially during or after competition. Post-game dinners or ice cream runs become the glue that holds the team together.

While there are always exceptions, boys tend to form relationships through the necessity of becoming teammates in order to prevail over common struggles.

The key takeaway is this: Regardless of gender, relationships are the foundation of every successful team. Consequently, as a coach, building trust and fostering connections should be a top priority.

Relationships Build Teams

When I first started coaching, I underestimated the importance of relationships. My focus was entirely on writing training plans and implementing strategies. I believed that if the workouts were sound, success would follow. What I failed to realize was that relationships determine whether athletes truly buy into the program.

In my first year as head coach for boys' cross-country, I inherited a team that had two wins and five losses in dual meets the previous season. I believed we had enough talent to improve, but I overlooked a critical detail: the disconnect between our younger athletes and the more experienced ones. It became clear that if we wanted to elevate our team, we had to create opportunities for bonding.

One of the most effective ways we did this was through competition. We often split the squad into smaller groups, making seniors captains and mixing up friend groups. With boys, nothing strengthens relationships quite like competition.

For the girls' teams, team bonding does not typically require a competitive element. In fact, some of the best girls' bonding experiences happen outside of traditional training. Team dinners, outings, and obstacle courses all help these athletes connect. One of the most memorable examples I've seen came from our girls' volleyball team. They visited a local crew boathouse and learned how to row together. Every athlete in this case was on an equally unfamiliar level, struggling and learning at the same time. It was a priceless experience that brought them closer as a team.

Looking back on my career, I realize I struggled at times like many coaches to keep my eye on what matters most: building positive relationships. I see a recurring blind spot in those early years, one that often showed up in the form of neglecting connections with my athletes or letting team dynamics falter behind the pursuit of talent or performance.

I learned the hard way that relationships matter more than any training plan. A great workout can build strength, but strong relationships are what build teams. But relationships don't form overnight. They require time, effort, and intentionality.

After practice, I make it a point to spend fifteen to thirty minutes talking with athletes. Those conversations, even if they seem trivial, can be transformative. We also have a simple rule: If teammates or coaches pass each other in the hallway, they must acknowledge each other with a greeting or high five.

A team that feels like a family will work harder, compete better, and handle setbacks with resilience. When athletes trust their teammates and coaches, they perform at their best. And a bonded team is hard to beat.

Athlete Profile: John Collins, Class of 2002

John Collins had some success before I arrived at East Kentwood, running a 17:23 for a cross-country 5k as a sophomore. That season was coached by my predecessor, who had originally recruited John's older brother—John had come along as a bit of a bonus.

John was a junior during my first year coaching cross-country. This was my first opportunity to be a head coach and run my own program. He was clearly talented but rarely trained in the summer and often took shortcuts during workouts. His inconsistent effort frustrated me, and I'll admit now that I wouldn't have been upset if he had chosen not to come out his senior year. I knew what he was capable of, but his preparation didn't match his potential. As a result, we butted heads often.

At the end of the season, following tradition from previous coaches, our team voted for the next year's captains. Much to my surprise—and honestly, my dismay—John was elected captain over two other solid athletes. At the time, I didn't have strong relationships with many of the athletes, so I suspected some had voted for John in spite of me. Looking back, their undermining choice was more about my inexperience and inflated ego than anything else.

After each season, we hosted a team banquet. It was a time to bring athletes and parents together, share a meal, and celebrate everything the team had accomplished. The banquet gave the coach a chance to highlight the season, thank the seniors for their leadership, and set the tone for what was to come next.

Within a few days of the banquet, I pulled John aside. I suggested he consider stepping down as captain—or even not returning for his senior year. I told him I was concerned that his work ethic and leadership style could hurt the team more than help. To this day, I cringe at my words during that conversation. It was a clear example of how little I understood the value of relationships at the time. My approach was purely transactional, not transformational.

I didn't see much of John that winter. During track season, I wasn't the distance coach—I worked primarily with pole vaulters—so we didn't cross paths much. But one meet from that spring stood out. John raced against Dathan Ritzenhein, the Rockford standout who had placed third in the world at the under-eighteen-year-old Cross-Country World Championships just a few months earlier. In that dual meet, John faced Dathan in the 800m—and while he didn't beat him, he pushed him. That moment lit a fire in John. Whether it was the result, the competition, or simply how he felt during the race, it clearly motivated him.

By the time summer rolled around, something had changed. John and the other captains created a summer training plan. It was simple but powerful: If a teammate didn't show up, they'd run to their house, knock on the door, and stay until that athlete joined. It was one of the first glimpses I had of the kind of leader John was becoming.

That summer transformed him. He trained harder, led louder, and inspired more. He was maximizing his talent, and for the first time, I felt like he truly believed in the process. But in my inexperience, I pushed him too hard. I had him running more miles than his body was ready for, and about three-quarters into the season, he developed a stress fracture from overuse. He had been an incredible leader and helped us become competitive in our Ottawa-Kent (OK) Red conference, but now he couldn't compete.

I feared he would check out, but he didn't. Instead, John became an unofficial assistant coach. He was at every practice and every meet, encouraging teammates, giving advice, and helping manage workouts. His leadership didn't waver. In fact, it grew. The same young man whose abilities to be captain I once questioned now had complete command of our team's culture.

John taught me more than I taught him. He showed me that relationships are more important than talent, and that building trust must start long before a season begins. His injury kept him off the course, but the culture he helped build carried us forward.

Before his injury, he had run 16:30 for a 5k, a very solid time for a high school runner, his best ever. He was poised for a breakthrough year before his injury. But even though his body gave out, his spirit never did.

John went on to have a successful senior track season, earned All-American honors at Grand Valley State University, and today works as a vice president at a local bank, still living in the area. He remains one of the most impactful leaders I've ever coached.

CHAPTER 5

Develop Leaders, Not Just Athletes

A leader is one who knows the way, goes the way, and shows the way.
—John C. Maxwell

I F I HAD to choose between developing leaders or athletes, the answer is easy: leaders.

When I began my coaching career, I heard that losing built character. I was not planning to coach a losing program so I knew I better invest some time in intentionally developing character. As a coach, I often wonder if the time we spend on character development could be better used refining skills or conditioning. Would an extra fifteen minutes a day working on technique make us more competitive? Probably. But without leadership, how could we exploit that small competitive edge and how productive would the rest of the day be outside of that quarter of an hour?

Coaching is full of stories of brilliant tacticians who struggle to win because their teams lack leaders. A prime example is the relationship between Tom Brady and Bill Belichick. Belichick, a certifiable football genius, struggled as a head coach until he had Brady—arguably one of the greatest leaders of all time. Together, they became the most dominant coach-player duo in NFL history. A sixth-round draft pick and a coach who was floundering at the time completely reshaped the league.

Even in programs without remarkable individual talent, there are still countless stories of average teams suddenly experiencing a standout season. When you look closely, the common denominator is always the same: an extraordinary leader who elevates the team's culture, sets the standard, and inspires their peers to follow.

The Importance of Leadership

Most coaches understand the rules and strategies of their sport. Some may know more than others, but this knowledge alone doesn't separate mediocre from good—or even good from great. Leadership is the key.

When your best athlete is also your best leader, success follows. But when your top athlete lacks leadership qualities, the team suffers—often at the worst possible times. I've had to confront this head-on, pushing talented athletes to either lead or step aside. If a star athlete can't or won't lead, they may need to defer to someone else. Or, in some cases, be removed from the team.

More than once, we have removed talented athletes from the team because they were unwilling to buy into the culture we have built. These are never easy decisions, but we cannot sacrifice the team for the poor choices of a few.

In most cases, when a highly talented athlete refuses to embrace the team culture, they end up suppressing the leadership potential of others. Once they are removed, something important often happens. New leaders rise, and the team reaches levels it could not reach before.

One of our core mantras is simple: Be great at the things that require no talent.

Show up on time. Be a good listener. Respect others. Do the small things well.

A good example of this mindset is our policy for away meets. If the bus is scheduled to leave at 11:15 a.m., it leaves at 11:15 a.m. Attendance is taken on the road at 11:20. If an athlete misses the bus, they do not compete that day. School policy requires athletes to take school transportation to contests. This rule teaches personal responsibility and commitment. Over the years, we have left athletes behind. We have even left coaches. I have made it clear that if I am ever late, the team should not even wait for me.

There have been times when we did not perform at our best after leaving a key athlete behind. But those athletes understood the consequences of being late and learned a valuable life lesson. Leadership begins with being present and being on time.

I have replaced talented athletes with true leaders. When a gifted athlete begins to lead the team in the wrong direction, hard choices must be made. Are we willing to trade team growth and unity for the sake of talent?

The answer is always no. Leaders win in the end.

Talent may open the door, but it is not enough on its own. When a team relies on athletes who lack leadership and character, failure becomes not only likely but inevitable. And when that failure arrives, it often comes at the worst possible time.

Hold your athletes accountable for all of their actions, especially when those actions affect the team. Because even in a sport like track and field, where athletes compete individually, it's leadership that brings teams to the top.

No Captains, Just Leaders

I haven't named captains on our track team in over twenty years. Instead, every Falcon is expected to lead. If you can't lead, you're expected to follow fiercely.

Selecting captains often causes more problems than it solves. Whether the athletes vote, the coaches choose, or there's an application process, the result is the same: resentment and jealousy. Over the years I have seen athletes completely shut down, become worse teammates and even threaten to transfer as a result of someone else being named captain. The title of captain can feel arbitrary, especially when there's no clear standout. I've seen otherwise completely sane and rational parents and athletes so upset over not being named captain that they considered transferring schools.

As an athletic director, I deal with this issue several times a year across various teams. My response is always the same: "How does your team change if you never name captains?" The answer is usually "not much." If there's no question about who the leaders are, titles don't matter. And if you lack leaders, naming captains doesn't fix the problem—it only highlights it.

Instead of captains, we have line leaders. With over 150 athletes on the team, we organize warm-ups into ten to twelve lines, with ten or more people per line. If someone steps to the front of the line, they're a leader. Anyone can create their own line and lead it. If people follow, great. If not, they can join another line. This simple system ensures that leadership is earned, not assigned. By midseason, leaders naturally emerge, and everyone knows who they are—no formal titles required.

Leaders on our team take on a few unofficial roles. They accept trophies on behalf of the team, hold teammates accountable, and set the tone in practice and competition. They do this not because they're assigned a title, but because they've earned the respect of their peers.

Athlete Profile: Job Mayhue, Class of 2018

Job Mayhue is one of the best leaders I've ever coached—mature beyond his years.

He grew up in downtown Grand Rapids but chose to attend Kentwood schools, which meant his parents had to drive him into our district each day. Occasionally, he took the city bus—an hour-long commute each way. He never mentioned needing a ride; he just used the bus so he wouldn't burden anyone.

That's just who Job was—quietly determined and unwilling to let circumstances define him.

Physically mature for his age, Job was already over six feet tall in middle school and eventually grew to six feet, three inches. He stood out wherever he went, and his natural charisma made him impossible to ignore. Teachers quickly learned that when Job was in their class, there would be joy, laughter, and most importantly, respect.

Job had a way of shifting the dynamic of any room for the better. He was a natural thermostat—regardless of the temperature when Job walked in, he adjusted it to fit the needs of the situation. If things needed to turn up, Job could bring the energy. If things needed to settle down, he knew how to do that too. He was constantly encouraging others, always looking out for people, and deeply invested in his teammates' well-being.

People always knew Job was there for them, whether they were at their best or struggling. He led through his genuine love for others. When he asked how you were doing, he truly meant it. He wanted to know. Beyond his natural leadership, Job was also incredibly intelligent. He was positive, well-liked, and respected by everyone around him.

As a hurdler coached mainly by Stephanie Stephenson, Job was a high school All-American and a state champion. But his considerable impact wasn't just on the track—it was on his teammates. He thrived on our daily character speeches, and his enthusiasm was contagious.

His presence elevated those around him, proving that leadership isn't about personal talent—it's about outward influence.

One day, during Job's senior year, there was a commotion in the crowded hallway near the fieldhouse. In a school of nearly 3,000 students, the hallways can get pretty crowded. Hundreds of students had gathered, and safety staff rushed in, assuming they would be breaking up a fight.

But by the time they arrived, nothing was happening. The crowd had dispersed, and everyone was back in class.

Suspicious, the staff reviewed the security footage. The video indeed showed two boys fighting, but then Job entered the frame. He grabbed both boys, separated them, and sent them in opposite directions. Turning to the crowd, he then told everyone to move along, and within seconds, the hallway was clear. The safety staff were impressed and called me to share the story. While I wasn't surprised, I was still incredibly proud. Job didn't lead for recognition—he led to make everyone around him better.

After graduating, Job attended the University of Michigan on a track scholarship, where he became a standout student-athlete. As a sophomore, he was admitted to the prestigious Ross School of Business. As a junior, he was named captain of the track team, earning more votes than any other athlete across all event groups.

Of course, the official title of captain hardly mattered; everyone already knew who the leader was. His coaches praised his ability to lead not just the hurdlers, but the entire team. His impact had always been undeniable.

Job Mayhue's story is a testament to the power of leadership that transcends individual talent—the kind of influence that leaves a positive lasting mark on everyone it touches.

CHAPTER 6

Trust the Process

The best way to predict the future is to create it.
—Peter Drucker

W HEN I THINK of the phrase "trust the process," I envision an *understanding* between coach and athlete. Trusting the process does not suggest blindly following; it means believing in the direction you are being led. The athlete is the driver of the car, responsible for effort, attitude, and execution. The coach holds the map, offering direction, perspective, and course corrections. Both roles matter, but the athlete is the one behind the wheel.

Of the hundreds if not thousands of athletes I have coached, I can honestly say I have not had much luck with kids who did not trust the process. If they truly didn't buy into our plan, their season or career never ended well. We've had talented kids who accomplished some of their goals, but a lack of trust eventually brought it all to an end—if not in high school, then in college.

I know it might sound odd coming from a team and staff who have accomplished so much, but we still spend an inordinate amount of time discussing our process to account for the "why" behind everything we do. We leave nothing to chance and work to erase as many doubts as we can. We speak about accomplishments, not to brag or impress, but to highlight the journeys other athletes have taken. Occasionally, we ask alumni to come back and share their experiences being on the team. They often encourage our current athletes to trust the coaching staff and seek guidance from their coaches. Sometimes, they even speak honestly about the times they did not trust the process and how they wish they had.

It is always an honor to have them with us. Their presence helps our athletes see where they are headed and reminds them that growth takes time—that there is something to learn from every experience. After all, if they have taken the trouble to return to our practice at their old high school, they must have something valuable to share.

Sometimes, this requires a reassessment on the part of the former Falcon, but perspective often comes with age. More often than not, athletes reflect on their struggles in high school, and their stories usually end with "I wish I had listened to the coaches more." Their voices wind up being far more powerful than ours could ever be.

Our Process

If I had to reflect on what defines our process for success, I would say it involves many things. It begins, of course, with a group of out-standing coaches who know their craft. Our staff can coach athletes in every discipline of our sport, and the standards for training and technique on our team remain high and consistent. However, when I truly consider what a successful "process" means to us, it goes far beyond mile repeats or perfect shot-put form.

The process is about growing as a complete person. It means showing up every day with an open mind, ready to learn something new. It involves understanding that your actions, and even your inactions, have an impact on the people around you.

The process is also about taking a journey together. It means recognizing that no one is perfect, but that we win together and lose together. There is no room for blame, whether directed at an athlete or a coach; there is only time to learn from mistakes and continue moving forward.

We ask athletes to trust the process by preparing each day with purpose, knowing that what they do today matters. It matters for their personal growth, their teammates, and the long-term goals of the program. This part of the process is about building relationships, investing in each other, and working together to create a culture that wins with consistency and character.

One message we repeat often is the importance of the word "us" in "trust the process." Many of our team shirts over the years have featured the letters *U* and *S* in bold. This is more than a design choice. It is a reminder to trust *us*. This means going beyond just trusting the coaches. Trust your teammates as well. Trust the effort. Trust the commitment. Trust the culture we are building together.

Have you ever wondered why some teams consistently excel while others struggle, even when the talent level appears similar? As coaches, we often hear debates from our athletes about who is better: Is it Michael Jordan or LeBron James? Tom Brady or Aaron Rodgers? Everyone has an opinion, and these discussions are endless.

But when you look deeper, one factor often distinguishes the legendary athletes: They trust the process.

As a coach fortunate enough to have won multiple state titles, I emphasize that team titles are the ultimate goal above personal achievement. Individual honors are great, but no one wants to be the best engineer at a failing company. It's about "the team, the team, the team," as Bo Schembechler famously said.

In Sam Walker's book *The Captain Class*, he highlights great sports dynasties and concludes that trust in the process is at the core of their success.[1] Athletes like Tom Brady bought into their coaches' vision—Brady trusted Bill Belichick implicitly—and he sold that process to their teammates. This dynamic was the foundation of their dominance. Without mutual trust, their achievements wouldn't have been possible.

Greatness in Comparison

Tom Brady vs. Aaron Rodgers

Both are legendary quarterbacks, but their paths couldn't be more different. Aaron Rodgers is undeniably more naturally talented—his arm strength and mobility are unmatched. Yet, Tom Brady has more Super Bowl wins than any quarterback in history. Why?

Again, Brady consistently trusted the process, a fact documented many times. Especially in the early years of growing a dynasty, Brady believed in the roadmap Belichick was drawing up. He let Belichick coach, bought into the system, and encouraged others to do the same. Rodgers, on the other hand, has clashed with multiple coaches over the years and struggled with buy-in from his teammates. The result? Rodgers has fewer championships despite his immense talent.

Michael Jordan vs. LeBron James

Michael Jordan and LeBron James are often compared in basketball, but their approaches differ considerably. Jordan trusted Phil Jackson's triangle offense and deferred to his coaches. This buy-in led to six NBA championships.

James, while undeniably one of the greatest, often acts as a coach on the floor, sometimes undermining systems by unilaterally taking

---

1 Sam Walker, *The Captain Class: The Hidden Force That Creates the World's Greatest Teams* (Random House, 2017).

control. He's won titles, but I believe his lack of consistent trust in the process has limited the sustained dominance we saw with Jordan's Bulls.

Trusting the Process in Coaching

When working with teenagers, trusting the process is at the heart of many conversations. Getting young athletes to buy into a plan—often one that includes hard work and discipline—is challenging. Many times, they have their own ideas, formed from the outside influence of friends, teachers, and especially parents. As a coach and athletic director, I can recall countless examples of talented athletes who did not trust the process and ultimately fell short of their goals. Eventually, every athlete must buy into what their coaches are teaching. Because even coaches who have not had a great deal of success can still offer valuable guidance if they have spent enough time in the sport.

Parents, in particular, play a crucial role in whether an athlete trusts the process. The parent who questions every coaching decision can quickly sow doubt in a young athlete's mind. A parent who trusts the process, however, reinforces the coach's message, creating a unified front that maximizes an athlete's potential.

What parents and athletes should always consider is that coaches work with dozens of athletes each year. They learn from every situation, constantly expanding their knowledge base. A parent may guide, at most, a few athletes over time, while the individual athlete, of course, has only their own experience to rely on. When parents think they know better and undermine a coach, they create chaos not only for their athlete but for the entire team. Nothing is accomplished through chaos.

Most parents have the goal of seeing their children pursue college athletics after high school. But if they were willing to undermine a high school coach, it's likely they will try to do the same to a college coach. On the pathway from club to high school to college athletics, patience is no longer trendy. It has become more common to readjust constantly, often giving up too soon on one program in search of the "right fit," but in doing so, the process of growth can be irretrievably lost.

Trusting your coaches and having faith that your efforts will pay off is crucial. In a sports world that feels increasingly transactional, where relationships are not nurtured over time, we will see plenty of highlights as spectators and participants—but far more lowlights will be left behind.

Over the years, I've noticed that athletes fall into four categories with regard to trusting the process:

1. **Athlete and parent buy in.** This is the ideal scenario. Both the athlete and parent trust the process, and the athlete maximizes their potential.
2. **Athlete doesn't buy in, but parent does.** This often leads to the athlete coming around eventually, as there's no external negativity influencing the athlete to undermine their coach.
3. **Athlete buys in, but parent doesn't.** This is challenging. If the parent voices their doubts, the athlete may lose trust during tough moments.
4. **Neither buys in.** This is a no-win situation and usually results in failure.

As coaches, it's our responsibility to bring athletes and parents on board. Success requires everyone rowing in the same direction. I have always worked hard to get parents on my side, and while this is often difficult to do, it's well worth the time and effort. Part of this process demands that the coach be an active member of the community, interacting with parents and acknowledging their role in building the program's culture of greatness. Toward this end, here are a few suggestions:

- Volunteer at Little League and other youth events.
- Be involved in your program from top to bottom, not just on the field.
- Learn who the parents are—some will have big personalities, and some will be natural leaders.
- Build relationships with parents when their kids are young; this will pay off when conflicts arise and you can leverage the preexisting rapport to help resolve them.
- Hold a face-to-face parent meeting before the season, even if everything could be handled with an email.
- Don't hesitate to pick up the phone when even the smallest issue arises.

Taking the time to address small issues early allows you to work together and resolve minor problems quickly. This helps build trust and also shows that you can be reasonable if real conflicts occur in the future.

Over the years, I have always used a direct approach with parents. If I hear a rumor that there is a conflict, I will go straight to the source and contact the parents. This usually results in one of two reactions:

1. They respect me for speaking directly to them.
2. They understand that I will not avoid issues—going forward, I will confront them head-on.

If a parent wants to stir up problems at that time, I make it clear to them that we will work together to resolve any issues.

Athlete Profile: Breanna Eveland, Class of 2002

As a young coach, I already knew the name Eveland. Her older siblings were phenomenal athletes, and Bre proved to be no different, even from an early age. As a freshman on the varsity volleyball team in the winter, she was a standout on our state championship team.

That spring, I spoke to her parents about the possibility of her trying pole vault, but Bre was committed to playing softball. After some back and forth, we accepted that she might choose another sport over track.

Then came the first day of spring practice. Bre was asked to try out for the JV softball team while some of her classmates were invited to varsity tryouts. That didn't sit well with her. The next day, she showed up at both softball and track practices. By the end of the week, she had made her decision to pole vault, and the rest was history.

We had just gained one of the best athletes—and two of the most supportive parents—we could ask for in our program. We were over the moon, excited about the challenge ahead. The question now: Could we develop this young lady into a great track athlete?

Pole vault is a hard and weird sport. If any event requires trust from a young athlete, it's this one. Yet I have always enjoyed the connections I've made with my pole vaulters, and I think the process of overcoming the common unfamiliarity with the event is part of the reason why. There has to be absolute faith in the process and belief in the coach, because at the end of the day, I'm asking them to pick up a fiberglass pole, run full speed, and throw themselves over a bar set far above their heads.

Bre and I had a strong connection that created this necessary faith.

She trusted me—a young coach who, at the time, didn't know nearly as much about coaching as I do now. And yet she bought into the process. We took things slow, focusing on foundational skills step by step, never taking on more than she could handle. Trust in pole vault isn't built overnight; it's gained with each progression, each small victory, each moment an athlete overcomes fear.

When you have an athlete like Bre who trusts the process, your true coaching ability is revealed. She was going to do whatever I told her to do, so I'd better know what I was talking about. One day, in our eagerness to improve, I pushed Bre beyond her ability at the time. I asked her to jump on a pole that was a little bigger than what she was used to. She trusted me, took the attempt, and—unfortunately—came down short of the pit, breaking her ankle.

Days like these make you question your worthiness as a coach.

If athletes are going to trust the process, the process had better be sound. By pushing her too far in that moment, I let Bre down, but she never wavered in her belief. Three weeks after the injury—still in a boot—she qualified for the state meet on her first and only jump of the competition. Bre was the epitome of "trusting the process."

Coming from a family of elite volleyball players, her parents expected her to follow in her sisters' footsteps. Choosing pole vault over volleyball in college wasn't exactly what they had envisioned. But Bre bet on herself to excel in a different, unfamiliar sport, and her parents moved past initial misgivings and ultimately gave her their full support.

She went on to Kansas State University to compete for legendary coach Cliff Rovelto. Cliff was a master coach, and Bre trusted him completely. One winter break, he sent her home with a training plan that included running the stadium stairs. Cliff never considered that there would be six inches of snow on those stairs, but Bre never questioned the process and worked through the difficulty.

Bre believed in the plan, in the work, and in herself. That unwavering belief led her to become a three-time NCAA bronze medalist, an All-American, and an American record holder in the women's decathlon. Her story isn't just about natural talent. It's about trusting the process, running stadiums in the snow, and removing roadblocks that others might have simply tolerated.

Breanna Eveland didn't just follow a path—she built her own.

CHAPTER 7

Attitude and Effort

Excellence is not a skill. It is an attitude.
—Ralph Marston

WHEN I MEET with a group of athletes, I often ask, "What can you control?" The responses vary, but we always come back to two things: attitude and effort.

As a high school athlete, there are countless factors beyond your control. Coaches dictate the schedule, training, and goals. Transportation, practice locations, and assistant coaching decisions are all out of your hands. Every day, athletes show up and face whatever circumstances arise, including unexpected changes. This can leave them feeling powerless about their personal impact on the team. And truthfully, many athletes might not agree with the plans the coaching staff creates even if they ultimately have to abide by them.

However, to maximize potential, an athlete must focus on what they *can* control: relentless effort and an infectiously positive, determined attitude.

When an athlete brings such an attitude to practice—one that supports the team and approaches every task eagerly, not begrudgingly—they set the tone for everyone around them. A positive attitude becomes contagious. People can feel that energy and are drawn to it. We all know the athlete who shows up every day with a smile. This person brings energy to the locker room and sets the tone for the entire team. We call these athletes "thermostats"—they don't just gauge the temperature in the room, they set it. They have the ability to bring the heat when intensity is needed and cool things down when tensions rise.

Every team has a thermostat, but for the coach, the key is giving them the power to lead. Put them in a leadership role—maybe they organize warm-ups or break down the team at the end of practice. Their attitude is their light, and we, as coaches, need to let it shine. They don't need to be the best athlete, but if they can influence the best athlete to bring a great attitude, the entire team benefits.

On the flip side, there are "thermometers"—athletes who simply gauge the temperature in the room and reflect it. If the day is going poorly, they make sure everyone knows it. Thermometers are not useful to the team; everyone has the ability to read the energy of a situation, but not everyone has the skills to change it.

Grow your athletes into thermostats—players who can turn a bad start into a strong finish. We've all seen teams struggle in the first half and come back strong in the second. Somewhere in that locker room, a thermostat stepped up and shifted the energy. It could have been a coach, but it's even more powerful when it's an athlete.

Teams full of athletes eager to learn and tackle challenges head-on are hard to beat.

The second controllable factor is relentless effort. It's difficult to measure effort in small doses, but maximal effort is unmistakable. When you give your all, there's no question about your heart being in it. Your teammates see it, feel it, and are forced to match your intensity—or risk being left behind.

Unfortunately, relentless effort can be challenging to maintain if the team culture doesn't support it. Teams with poor culture are often critical of "try-hards," often targeting them as too performative or anxious to please. But I have never met a coach who wouldn't love to coach a team full of try-hards. Maximal effort should always be encouraged and rewarded.

Sometimes your best athlete doesn't have the best attitude or doesn't give great effort every day. In those cases, your presumed leader may lead you away from a desired outcome by modeling slack behavior. If talent or privilege outweighs effort in your team's culture, it can be a struggle to make the switch and foster a culture of relentless effort and thermostatic attitudes. But attitude and effort will always pay off—in athletics, at work, and in life. The story of the talented athlete who never accomplished much—either in sports or in life—has been told over and over again. In fact, everyone knows an underperforming uncle, neighbor, or coworker who scored four touchdowns for Polk High.

Attitude and effort buttress all aspects of life. Teach these critical skills to all athletes, not just the stars. Athletes who bring a great attitude and relentless effort every single day may not always become the best, as talent still plays a role, but they will impact the team far beyond the scoreboard.

Athlete Profile: Amanda Impellizeri, Class of 2009

Amanda joined the pole vault crew as a freshman, and to be honest, she wasn't very good. In her entire freshman season, she cleared a bar in only one meet. She "no-heighted" in every other meet, failing three times at the opening height. Amanda didn't contribute to the team her first year, but to my surprise, her name was still on the roster her sophomore year. I even encouraged her to try other events.

In response, she took up discus but refused to quit pole vaulting. And every day, Amanda brought an incredible attitude to practice. She failed repeatedly but never let it shake her spirit. She smiled through every setback, inspiring the rest of the team. Because if Amanda wasn't complaining, how could anyone else?

As a sophomore, she made more progress but was still not exceptional. However, her relentless effort and positivity started to influence the entire pole vault crew. By her junior year, Amanda had become a solid competitor, clearing eleven feet and earning All-State honors. When Amanda was on our team, not only did she improve every day, but every pole vaulter around her improved every day. Because her attitude was infectious. Each day, Amanda came to practice with a smile. I cannot recall a time in four years when she was outwardly sad or unwilling to laugh at a joke—even if it was at her own expense. Everyone around her felt like they were in her orb of influence; no one felt left out or unseen. I know for a fact that we maximized our team during this time.

Her senior year, Amanda improved again, scoring points in both pole vault and discus. She had always planned to attend Michigan State University and asked me about walking onto their track team. I doubted whether it was the right move, thinking maybe she had maxed out what attitude and effort could achieve.

I was wrong.

Amanda joined MSU's track team and thrived. Despite being surrounded by more talented teammates, she rose to the top through her work ethic and positivity. By the end of her college career, Amanda was the school record holder in the women's pole vault.

Amanda and Coach Emeott forming a plan (Photo by Jim Swoboda)

CHAPTER 8

The One

The strength of the team is each individual member.
The strength of each member is the team.
—Phil Jackson

A S OUR TEAM ascended toward greatness in the early years of my career, we grew closer each season. We built relationships, strengthened our culture, and pursued a state title together. Everyone was on board, and we were so proud of the team we were becoming. We were on the verge of something epic, and it felt like everyone around us knew it.

At the 2007 state finals, we finished as runners-up to Ann Arbor Pioneer, losing 28 to 46. Despite the loss, bringing home a trophy was a monumental achievement, and the excitement reverberated throughout our school. Our superintendent even bought us a new pole vault pit to celebrate our best finish ever.

The following year, we weren't just looking to compete—we were determined to win. We believed we had a stronger team, and it felt like nothing could stop us. Yet, when the dust settled, we came up just short, losing by the narrowest of margins: 55 to 56. Scoring 55 was an incredible feat—it was the highest total ever for a team that didn't win a state title. Most years, state champions won with scores in the forties. But on that day, Flint Carman-Ainsworth was just one point better than us.

The entire 2009 offseason became an obsession with that single-point loss. We dissected every race, every event, and every possible moment where we could have earned just one more point. As coaches, we were haunted by one question: "What could we have done differently?" That offseason, we worked harder than ever. Every practice, meeting, and training session was driven by one singular focus:

Find one more point.

In mid-February, tragedy struck. Our beloved sprint coach, Bob Eubanks, passed away suddenly from a heart attack. Bob was a legend in the Grand Rapids area. Even before his passing, both a high school and a college invitational bore his name, honors that are usually bestowed posthumously. His loss was a profound shock to the entire team.

Days after the news, we found ourselves at Bob's funeral, mourning a man who had not only helped build this team but had also formed deep connections with everyone. Suddenly, what seemed important before—winning for the sake of winning—now felt trivial. Our purpose shifted, and that season, we dedicated everything we would achieve to Coach Eubanks.

Our team motto that year—"The One"—originally referred to that one point we lost by. It was no longer about that one point or the title we didn't win; it was now about Coach Eubanks. His memory became the cornerstone of our season. Every sprinter wrote "The One" on their shoes, and our team gear reflected the same theme. We trained, competed, and pushed ourselves to honor him.

The team became unstoppable. One day, during a tornado warning, all after-school activities were canceled, and everyone was sent home—including me. Around 3:30 p.m., about an hour after the evacuation, a safety officer called me, furious. Our kids had snuck into a back stairwell at school to get a workout in. Although I couldn't outwardly say so (and obviously can't condone it now), I couldn't have been prouder at the time.

The team dominated every meet, led by an extraordinary sprint group that eventually scored 57 at the state meet. The team's total of 79 was the highest ever scored at a Division I state meet at that time—more than second and third place combined. East Kentwood had won its first track and field state title in school history, and we proudly dedicated the entire season to Coach Eubanks.

That year, I saw kids fight for something far greater than trophies. I witnessed how tragedy could fuel focus and determination. I know Coach Eubanks was incredibly proud of those young men.

Creating Themes That Matter

I would never wish tragedy upon a team. It was an incredibly difficult time for our kids, and even in victory, we grieved the loss of a great man. However, I believe it is important to work hard to create themes for each season—something that unifies and drives your team beyond just competition.

What are your goals? Your theme could be built around your team's success, but it doesn't have to be limited to that. It might have nothing to do with winning or losing and instead focus on building a strong, lasting culture.

One of my favorite themes, which I've used multiple times over the years, is former UCLA basketball coach John Wooden's "Pyramid of Success." The pyramid consists of fifteen building blocks, each representing a fundamental trait of success.[2] I print each one on a

---

2 The pyramid is organized as follows: At the base are Industriousness, Friendship, Loyalty, Cooperation, and Enthusiasm. Above the base are Self-Control, Alertness,

half sheet of paper and introduce a new concept daily, first sharing Wooden's explanation and then adding my own twist.

To keep the material fresh, I revisit the Pyramid of Success every four years, ensuring no athlete sees it more than once during their time in our program. I encourage every coach to explore Wooden's Pyramid of Success and consider how its principles could shape their team—not just for a season, but for life.

Athlete Profile: Tyrone Green, Class of 2009

Tyrone Green was raised by his mother, while his father lived in another state and was not involved. Tyrone was the youngest of three children. His mother worked long hours to support him and his older siblings, doing everything she could to provide for their needs. Tyrone was the only one who pursued athletics, and he struggled in school, rarely earning good grades. He admits now that he often saw himself as the central protagonist in every situation, something he calls "Main Character Syndrome." He pushed back on rules and structure, seeing the world through a lens that centered around himself.

As a sophomore in 2007, he showed promise but struggled with discipline and missed the postseason due to academic and behavioral issues. As a junior, he became our best sprinter, coached by Tim Stenceil, but he still did not buy into the team-first mentality that defines our program.

One of our core values is celebrating as a team. We don't believe in solo victories. Even in individual wins, we expect athletes to look for a coach or teammate to share the moment with. Shake an opponent's hand. Congratulate them on their effort. Be intentional about what it means to be a Falcon in victory.

Tyrone didn't understand that—and at the time, he didn't care. He won league titles and dominated meets, but his chest-pounding celebrations and over-the-top antics often alienated teammates. When

---

Initiative, and Intentness. Next up are Condition, Skill, and Team Spirit. Above that are Poise and Confidence. Finally, at the top of the pyramid is Competitive Greatness.

relays broke down, he deflected blame instead of taking responsibility. As the fastest sprinter in the program, his behavior drew attention and began to affect the entire sprint squad in a negative way.

Kevin Jackson, a respected team leader, tried to address the issue privately. Kevin usually had a way of persuading teammates to adjust, but Tyrone wasn't interested. Frustrated, Kevin came to me and said, "We will never win with that kind of stuff on our team."

I told him, "This is your team as much as it is mine. If you think he's a problem, you make the call." Together, we agreed to give Tyrone one more chance. I met with him personally, made the team's expectations clear, and let him know this wasn't just my stance—it was how his teammates felt too. I trusted Kevin's leadership. He had proven himself to be one of the best leaders we'd ever had, and his passion for success was unmatched.

The breaking point came a week later at the OK Red Conference Championships. Despite repeated warnings, Tyrone celebrated another win with a loud, theatrical display. After a dominating 100-meter dash, he put on a show. But instead of looking for teammates to celebrate with or shaking an opponent's hand, the moment was all about him.

That wasn't the image we wanted. Celebration wasn't the problem—selfish celebration was. If Tyrone had included his teammates, we would've welcomed it. But the "look at me" routine wasn't what our program stood for.

With counsel from Kevin and other leaders, I made the difficult decision: Tyrone was off the team. The next day, I broke the news to him. He begged to return, but the decision was final.

We ended up losing the state meet that year by a single point—a point Tyrone might have earned. But we never second-guessed the choice. Some things are more important than winning.

That moment became a turning point in our program. We made it clear: Winning was not the ultimate goal. Putting the team before self was the goal. Growth and transformation were the goals.

Redemption and Growth

As I had promised the previous year, Tyrone had the opportunity to return his senior year, and he took it. Over the offseason, we had several conversations. I told him we hadn't given up on him, but he had to change. This wasn't just about track and field; it was about learning life lessons. When he returned in 2009, Tyrone was a different person. He embraced the team-first mentality and became a mentor to younger athletes, including Jon Henry, one of the most talented runners in school history.

At the state finals, both Tyrone and Jon Henry qualified for the 100-meter final. Jon had never beaten Tyrone, but he looked strong that day. Throughout the prelims and semis, Jon and Tyrone were never head-to-head but were dominant against the rest of the field. Our coaching staff believed that Jon looked like he was poised to beat Tyrone for the first time. I worried about how Tyrone would handle a loss, especially if it came from a younger teammate. I stood near the finish line, unsure what to expect.

The race started, and from the first step, it was clear East Kentwood would capture first and second place. When it ended, Tyrone turned, hugged Jon, and then ran over to me shouting, "Coach, we went 1-2! Can you believe it?" I asked, "Who won?" He said, "Not sure. Doesn't matter. We went 1-2."

In that moment, I saw just how far he had come. Tyrone finally understood the value of team over self. It was one of the most powerful transformations I have ever seen in a student-athlete.

Today, Tyrone lives in our community. His daughter now runs on the middle school team. He works as a truck driver and crew supervisor for a local bakery. I cannot say that track alone changed his life, but I know we tried our best, and I am proud of the man he has become.

In my interview for this book, Tyrone told me being part of the team was the greatest experience of his life. The lessons he learned didn't take hold right away, but over time, they did. He told me they were like seeds that eventually bloomed as he matured. That might be one of the greatest compliments I have ever received.

Tyrone accepting the baton from Kody Dantuma (Photo by Jim Swoboda)

CHAPTER 9

Control the Controllables

Do what you can, with what you have, where you are.
—Theodore Roosevelt

I N LIFE, SUDDEN changes are inevitable, and control is a privilege we rarely have. As coaches, we must learn to quickly assess situations, identify what we can control, and move forward. Many aspects of athletics are beyond our control—facilities, weather, opponents, and even recognition of our athletes' achievements by the media, the community, or larger athletic organizations. But wasting energy on things outside our influence only detracts from what we can control.

As a coach, I've experienced this firsthand, particularly with controversies like bad calls from officials. One of the best lessons I learned about dealing with officiating came from my good friend and long-time basketball coach, Jeff Anama. East Kentwood is an incredibly diverse school, and sometimes, when we played less diverse teams, it felt like officials were biased. I'd vent to Jeff, saying, "That guy always screws us!" Jeff would calmly respond, "He isn't good. He's not biased; he's just not very good."

While I didn't entirely buy into his perspective, and I am not always sure Jeff did either, his larger point stuck with me: We can't control the officials, so why waste energy trying?

As a track coach, my sport offers a unique perspective: Unlike football, baseball, or basketball, there's no defense. We can't control our opponents or their performance through defensive maneuvers. Furthermore, we can't control where we are located and whom we compete against. The OK Red, our conference, is one of the toughest in Michigan. While we'd likely win more meets in another league, we simply are where we are on the map. However, we can control how we respond to challenges and prepare our team to succeed.

In 2010, the night before the state championship meet, I invited a few members of the 2009 team to speak to our athletes. One of those former athletes was Tyrone Green, who had gone on to run junior college track in Texas. He gave an incredible speech about his time on the team, the growth he experienced, and how it changed his life. The athletes were on the edge of their seats.

After he finished, he gave me a big hug—one of the best feelings in the world. Then he asked, "Did you give them the letters yet? Those letters were really life-changing."

My heart dropped. I felt like a fool.

For the past two years, I had started a tradition: writing a personal letter to every athlete who qualified for the state meet. I would hand it to them in the locker room the day before the meet and ask them to read it when they were alone, not sharing the message until after the competition. Each letter was printed on a page with the EK logo watermarked behind the words.

In 2008, before we had won anything, the letters were more like short notes. In 2009, I started writing full letters—two to three paragraphs long. The first half was a personal message from me to them, reflecting on our journey together, how proud I was of them, and how much they had grown. The second half was a step-by-step script for their state meet day.

But in 2010, I hadn't written the letters.

I had always viewed these letters as a way to push our kids over the top—to help them win. And in 2010, it seemed like we didn't need the help. We were by far the best team in the state, and I knew we were going to cruise to another title. Without even realizing it, I had been transactional about these letters. I thought they were just another strategy to make us more competitive, and because of our dominance that year, they seemed dispensable.

Until I spoke to Tyrone.

That's when I realized the letters were much more than a road map to victory. They were love letters. They were my way of telling these kids how much I cared about them—something many of them didn't hear very often. When Tyrone asked the question, I knew I was cooked. I hadn't even considered writing them.

As soon as practice was over, I knew what I had to do. What should have been a night of celebration turned into an all-nighter. We had over twenty kids going to the meet the next morning: seventeen individuals, most of them seniors, plus members from all four relay teams.

The letters were controllables, and I had lost control. After a quick meeting with the coaching staff, I went home and started writing. As a math teacher who dealt infrequently with composition, writing these letters was probably the hardest thing I did each year. They usually took me weeks to prepare, and now I had twelve hours. I worked all night. Then, when I finally hit print, my home printer wasn't working. Frantic, sweating, and exhausted, I had to go into school early Saturday morning—after the school year had ended—to find a printer. It was a mad scramble, but I got it done. I barely had time for a quick shower before jumping on the bus with letters in hand.

As I walked to the back of the bus, my shorts caught on the edge of a starting block one of the kids had brought. They ripped completely—from midway up the zipper to the bottom of the leg. This state meet day was not off to a great start.

But when I started handing out the letters, I saw the surprise on their faces.

"Oh wow, Coach, I thought you forgot."

"I didn't think you were doing them this year."

"Thank you, Coach. I loved my letter last year—I can't wait to read this one."

The day played out in historic fashion, and we won. We scored ninety-two points, the most ever in the history of Michigan by any Division 1 team. In the weeks that followed, I attended many graduation parties for those young men. On their display tables—next to their medals, trophies, and pictures—were those letters.

The letters that almost didn't happen. The letters I had once thought were simply about winning. The letters that truly told them how much I cared about them as people.

Ripped shorts and broken printers were uncontrollables. But traditions and standards—those are controllable.

Always control the controllables.

Athlete Profile: Evert Geerlings, Class of 2008

The day I signed my contract to teach at East Kentwood High School was also the first time I met Evert Geerlings. I was at lunch with my principal, John Brillhart, and across the restaurant was Evert with his father and two younger brothers—just three little boys hanging out with their dad. Evert's father, Kurt Geerlings, was a legend in EK track and field lore—our school record holder in the pole vault and one of the top vaulters in the country during his prime. He was also the current pole vault coach at EK.

Sadly, Kurt battled alcoholism and eventually became estranged from his family. That's a much longer story, but the result was this: About six months after I started at EK, Kurt was removed as pole vault coach, and I stepped in to take over the event.

Evert's mom, Julie, raised the three boys on her own. She is an incredible woman—strong, dedicated, and full of grace—and she raised three remarkable kids. I actually tried to recruit Evert to pole vault when he was in fifth grade (probably three or four years after I had started coaching), but he wanted nothing to do with me—and absolutely nothing to do with the pole vault. I didn't blame him; I probably would have reacted the same way. After his initial refusal, I didn't reconnect with him again until his freshman year.

Evert's story hit close to home for me. We shared a similar upbringing—both raised by single mothers after difficult relationships with alcoholic fathers, both the oldest of three brothers. For me, working with Evert became more than just coaching. It was a labor of love. There were moments when I felt a connection with Evert that was deeper than the typical coach-athlete relationship—closer even than comparable moments I've had with my own children. We connected then, and we still connect today on so many levels.

Recruiting Evert to pole vault wasn't easy. I approached him during his freshman year in his math class, which was across the hall from mine. He was older and a little bigger than he had been in fifth grade, and this time, for some reason, he relented and came out for the track team.

At first, he still wanted no part of a sport so closely tied to his father's mixed legacy. But as high school went on, I think part of him quietly hoped he could make sense of that piece of his story—to connect, in some small way, to the father he'd grown distant from. Pole vault became that outlet.

By the time Evert was a senior, his father Kurt was incarcerated, although he would be released to a halfway house that year in time for the track season. Though they had no contact, Kurt did attend a few meets, watching quietly from a distance. I remember one time Kurt called me—emotional and proud—telling me how impressed he was with Evert's progress. He couldn't help offering a few technical tips, too. Due to the no-contact order by the courts, this was verging on inappropriate conversation, but I let him speak. A few months later, Kurt relapsed into alcoholism and passed away—a tragic ending to a complicated and painful story.

And yet, through all of it, Evert became the living definition of this chapter's theme: Control the controllables. I'm sure, deep down, there was always the hope that his dad would return or that they could one day share a relationship. Through Kurt's death, once again, Evert was dealt a blow that was completely outside of his control.

What he *could* control, however, was his response to tragedy. And every single day, he showed up and gave his all. He brought relentless effort to every practice. He wasn't the most naturally gifted athlete on the team, but he was a born leader. His energy was contagious, and his consistency and character became cornerstones of our culture.

That year, our team won the Michigan Interscholastic Track Coaches Association (MITCA) team state championship—a title that celebrates depth and team-wide contribution, not just individual talent. Evert's leadership and influence, along with that of several teammates, helped lay the foundation for the many state titles that followed.

After graduation, Evert attended Calvin College, where he continued to pole vault and earned a degree in sports management. As you can imagine, that's a tough field to break into. Everyone wants to work in the NFL. The path is grueling—usually unpaid internships, long hours, and very little recognition.

Evert embraced the grind.

He interned with the Detroit Lions for a season, then with the New York Jets, and later with the Oakland Raiders. To make it all work financially, he'd return home between NFL seasons and work factory jobs for six months at a time—just to save enough money to go back and chase the next opportunity. Most people would've given up.

Evert doubled down.

Eventually, his persistence paid off. He earned a full-time role with the Las Vegas Raiders, and from there, his career continued to rise. Then, Evert served as the senior football communications manager for the Houston Texans, and at the time of writing this book, he has been named the youngest vice president in the NFL, where he will take on the role of vice president of football communications for the Tennessee Titans.

His story is a blueprint for this chapter—living proof that even when life throws the uncontrollable your way, *what you choose to do with your attitude, effort, and integrity still matters and is still under your sway.*

So much of Evert's life was outside of his control. But the parts he *did* have power over? He executed them with purpose, clarity, and vision. Step by step. Brick by brick.

I'm so proud of Evert—and I hope his story inspires others the way it continues to inspire me.

Evert Geerlings and the vault crew! (Front row, from left to right: Zack Vanderwall, Kyle Helzer, Evert, Robbie Rix, Brian Akers. Above them, wearing sunglasses: Coach Emeott.)

CHAPTER 10

Rules Are Rules

*Discipline is choosing between what you want
now and what you want most.*
—Abraham Lincoln

WHEN I WAS a young coach, I believed one rule was enough: respect. Respect everyone, and everything else will fall into place—or so I thought. This worked well enough until real issues arose. Conflict and rule-breaking exposed the flaws in such a vague policy. Respect alone didn't give us the tools to address problems, deliver consequences, or guide behavior effectively.

These days, athletes are rarely alone when issues arise on your team. Any time you are ready to enforce a consequence for an athlete's actions, you can almost guarantee it will be questioned by a parent. Coaches must document incidents and be able to defend their actions. It's not fun, but it does provide a level of checks and balances. It also requires coaches to be diligent and clear about expectations.

For example, every coach should have a consistently enforced attendance policy with explicit reasons for varied consequences—because if you don't, it will be tested.

"Why can Jenny miss practice and still play, but when I miss, I have to sit?"

Are you prepared to answer that question?

On our team, we have a strict "no swearing" policy. We do not swear—ever. The consequence for violating this policy is simple: twenty-five push-ups. Anyone on the team can enforce it. Even the lowest-ranking freshman can call out their coach on the spot, requiring immediate push-ups from the offender. From time to time, I've had old-school football coaches on my staff, and they tend to struggle with two things: language and push-ups.

After one particular meet, I was upset. The team was sitting in the bleachers listening to me rant about something like lack of self-discipline and poor attitudes. In my frustration, I said, "What the hell are we doing?"

Now, in my personal life, I probably swear too much. I am fully capable of using all the words. But when I'm working with kids, that's not the time or place. The moment "hell" left my mouth, I heard a ninth grader from the back murmur, "Push-ups." Immediately, I dropped to the ground, took my consequence, and continued with my speech. But at that point, I had lost all momentum. The whole group sat there with huge smiles on their faces. Who lacked discipline in that moment?

What are your rules? Be specific, have clear consequences, and be ready for anything.

The Reading of the Laws

The turning point for my rules philosophy came at a cross-country clinic, where I heard legendary Pinckney High School coach Tom

Carney speak about his team's rules. His list of fifty wasn't vague; it was detailed, specific, and practical. Some rules addressed behavior, others offered advice, and a few even injected humor. Inspired, I asked if I could borrow his list, and he agreed. (By "borrow," I mean steal a great idea from a great coach.)

Over the years, we've credited Tom many times as the foundation for our "Team Laws." His original fifty rules became our starting point, but we adapted them to reflect the unique challenges and values of East Kentwood. Writing these rules became a therapeutic process, allowing us to address frustrations and set clear expectations for behavior, attitudes, and team culture. This also allowed us to poke fun at ourselves from time to time. Self-deprecation can be a powerful tool.

At the beginning of each season, we gather the team to read through our Team Laws. The list has grown to over one hundred rules, covering everything from conduct during meets to proper uniform etiquette.

The reading takes about fifteen minutes. We pause occasionally to explain why certain rules exist. For example, "Don't knock over hurdles on purpose. Right, Mike?" was added one year because, the previous season, Mike attempted to run under a hurdle. These anecdotes informing the rules help the team understand the context behind each one and the importance of adhering to them. All actions have consequences.

Every athlete and parent receives a copy of the rules, both in hard copy and electronically. We've learned that clarity is critical for teenagers. The rules are a road map to success, and they leave little room for misinterpretation. The message is simple: Being on this team comes with guidelines. If you're not prepared for the consequences of breaking them, think carefully about your actions.

We follow a philosophy similar to the "Broken Windows Theory." In the early 1980s, when crime was surging in New York City, Mayor Rudy Giuliani and his administration began focusing on small offenses like vandalism and broken windows. The idea was that if you addressed the small problems, you could create an orderly environment that discouraged worse crimes from happening. Whether the theory is historically perfect or not, we believed the principle could work for us. At EK Track and Field, we sweat the small stuff.

In our program, no broken rule goes unnoticed or unaddressed. If everyone is held accountable for every small act of disrespect or disregard, no one ever feels singled out. Over time, this creates a culture of fairness, discipline, and shared responsibility.

East Kentwood Track Team Laws

You can find our current Team Laws in this book's appendix. You may feel that some of these rules seem silly or resemble broader life lessons, but the point is that we have expectations for behavior. Punishments for violating rules are purposefully left off the list, because while some of our rules come with hard and fast consequences, others will be handled more thoughtfully, in a way that is both fair and situationally appropriate.

Rules must be enforced fairly—but not always equally.

For instance, sitting an athlete on the bench might be devastating for one player, while another, who rarely plays or doesn't enjoy competing, might actually prefer sitting out. Maybe that athlete wants to avoid the embarrassment of a loud parent in the stands. In these cases, punishments for the two athletes may vary, but either way, a coach must make the consequence fit the situation. The goal is not just to punish but to change behavior.

Sometimes, punishment can be as simple as a conversation. Other times, you will need to drop the hammer. Some rules—like attendance and cursing—leave little room for gray areas. But for many rules, context must always be considered. Because in reality, life is full of gray areas and special circumstances. The key is to be consistent and fair in how you handle every situation.

Each rule serves a purpose, whether it's building character, promoting discipline, or fostering team unity. As coaches, parents, and athletes, we can only succeed when we understand the framework in which we operate—and commit to following it.

Athlete Profile: Katie Rancourt, Class of 2012

Katie Rancourt's story embodies both the importance of rules and the grace required when they're broken.

Katie came from an athletic family. Her older brother, Phil, was an All-State pole vaulter who went on to compete at the Air Force Academy. Katie was an extraordinary athlete from a young age, excelling in soccer and competitive dance. I was eager to recruit her for the track team, but soccer seemed like the obvious choice for such a talented player.

Then, fate intervened. Katie's other brother, Richie, was cut from the soccer team. Katie loved Richie and was just as heartbroken as he was. Suddenly, soccer didn't seem as cool to her anymore. This opened the door for Katie to seriously consider pole vaulting, and I knew I had to pour on the charm to get her on our team.

My family and I had built a strong relationship with Katie's family through coaching her older brother. I knew early on that I wanted to recruit her to join our team someday, but I also knew it would take time and effort to build that connection.

When Katie was in sixth grade, she starred in a local theater production of *Junie B. Jones*, playing the role of "That Girl Grace." Coincidentally, *Junie B. Jones* was one of my daughter Macey's favorite books, and part of our nightly reading routine. Naturally, we were all excited to attend the show.

My family and I sat in the front row, holding a bouquet of flowers, ready to cheer her on. Katie was thrilled to see us, and we were completely entertained from start to finish. She stole the show that night. Her version of That Girl Grace was a high-energy, athletic interpretation that even included doing backflips on stage. It was a perfect preview of the kind of presence and talent she would later bring to our team.

Eventually, Katie chose track and left soccer behind. Here, I must pause and say, "Sorry, John" (John Conlon, our longtime legendary soccer coach and my great friend). Once she joined, Katie's tenacity and drive were unmatched. She quickly became a leader, both on the track and in our family; she babysat our kids and grew to be a close friend to my wife and children. My kids looked up to Katie like she was a goddess. She is probably one of the biggest reasons they became pole vaulters themselves.

Katie was a phenomenal athlete, but her life wasn't as perfect as it appeared. Her parents were heading toward divorce, and their remaining unity after the breakup often seemed to hinge on supporting Katie through graduation. In the end, her parents were among the most amazing, supportive parents we have ever had. They were always there to help in any way they could. In some cases, it's best to split rather than endure a fraught, potentially destructive marriage, and that's what happened here. Katie, unfortunately, was just caught in the middle. But despite these challenges, she thrived, which is a tribute to her, her amazing parents, and a strong family.

Then, on the night of senior prom, Katie made a mistake. The group she had gone to prom with were caught drinking alcohol during the dance. Security cameras captured them sneaking out to the car several times. That night, I received a call from the principal informing me of an incident we needed to discuss, but he didn't give me any details over the phone.

Driving to the school, I braced myself to hear the name of one of my male athletes. When I heard it was Katie, my heart sank.

Katie's punishment included a weeklong suspension and the loss of 20 percent of her season. During her suspension, I wasn't allowed to contact her, and I spent the week fuming without an outlet. I had planned to express my disappointment and lecture her on sabotaging her team and her future. At the end of the week, I was allowed to have a meeting with her and her family in their home. But when I walked into her kitchen, I was met with a broken young woman. Slumped at the table, unable to look me in the eyes, Katie tearfully apologized. She wasn't concerned about her suspension or her scholarship—her biggest concern was her obligation to the team and the staff. She knew she had let them down, and she was crushed.

Our house had become a refuge for her. Our children were like her siblings. But in that moment, she thought it was all over.

That was when I realized the importance of clear rules. The situation wasn't personal; it was about actions and consequences. I reassured Katie that while she had made a mistake, it didn't define her. She would serve her punishment, apologize to her team, and move forward.

Katie handled the situation with grace, taking full responsibility for her actions. She went on to win an MHSAA state title in pole vault and earn All-State honors in relays. She also received a scholarship to the University of Nebraska–Lincoln; her admission was the start of a great relationship between EK and UNL.

Today, she remains one of the best people I know—a testament to how rules, consequences, and second chances can shape character. Katie is still a valued member of our family, and we are happy to see her as often as we do.

Everyone makes mistakes. How we handle them is what matters most.

Katie Rancourt floating over the bar. Photo by Peter Draugalis

CHAPTER 11

If You Lie . . .

Honesty is a very expensive gift. Don't expect it from cheap people.
—Warren Buffett

G ROWING UP, MY stepdad always said, "If you lie, you'll cheat, and if you cheat, you'll steal." At the time, I didn't fully appreciate those words. But as I got older, I realized that honesty truly is the best policy, no matter the situation.

My high school track coach, Coach Frank, was the most honest person I've ever met. You didn't ask for his opinion unless you were ready for the unfiltered truth—good or bad. He was brutally honest, and sometimes it stung, but you always knew where you stood with him. That kind of honesty built a foundation of trust, and I have always tried to emphasize this fact in my coaching.

The Importance of Trust

I've always told my athletes, "I'll believe whatever you tell me. But the moment you lie to me, I'll never fully trust you again. From that point on, every word you say will need to be verified." I remind them that their actions today will shape how others view them for years to come. Someday, if they're selling tires and I'm the customer, I'll be thinking, "Is this the same kid who lied to me in high school?"

Your reputation for honesty follows you everywhere. While people can change and grow, regaining lost trust is a long road. As a coach, I aim to raise young people who choose the hard truth over the easy lie. It's not always easy to hold yourself to that standard and remain open to blunt, honest feedback. But if you do, expect to be held accountable as well.

There will be times when a kid says something like, "I didn't like the workout today. It felt the same as yesterday. I think we should've rested." That kind of feedback can be hard to hear without snapping back. But if you want honesty, you have to be able to take it. Train yourself to respond calmly, "I appreciate the feedback. Let's talk about it."

Honesty Is a Two-Way Street

If you're going to be a leader who values honesty, understand that it's a two-way street. Athletes look up to you. They believe in you. And often, they want to be like you. I ask my athletes to be honest with me—even if it means telling me things I don't want to hear. That's part of being a transformational coach: inviting truth, even when it hurts.

Young athletes who are successful in school, sports, and life are often very good at "playing the game." They know what to say and how to say it. But that doesn't mean they're being real with you. They're worried about how they'll be perceived, and sometimes they hold back. To get to the truth, you need to build strong, trusting relationships. And when they do open up—especially if it's about you or your program—you have to be ready. Even if what they say isn't the reality of the situation, it's their *perception* of truth, and perception is their reality—truth as they know it.

Don't shy away from it. Lean into it.

If you're going to ask them to be real with you, then you have to be strong enough to hear it without judgment. Sometimes athletes, for example, will say incredibly selfish things when they're being honest. That's part of the journey. Your job is to meet them where they are and help guide them toward where they need to be. Don't judge their feelings—teach them how to grow.

Communicating with Parents

Parents need honesty too. No surprise—they're usually focused on their own child first, and the team second. That's human nature. But if you can be clear that your decisions are based on what's best for the *team*, they'll at least understand your perspective even if they don't always agree.

Integrity in all situations will be your guiding light.

Of course, not all feedback is valid. Sometimes an athlete or parent might say something completely off base and anomalous. That's where experience helps. Lean into the feedback from the majority and take anything on the fringe with a grain of salt. In the end, it's honesty—no matter how difficult—that makes you a better coach, a better leader, and a better person.

Athlete Profile: Gabi Leon, Class of 2017

Gabi was the youngest of five children, raised primarily by her strong mother in a divorced household. She came to EK from a local charter school where track and field wasn't even offered. Gabi had played the spring season of JV soccer as a freshman, and had just wrapped up a season of JV volleyball as a sophomore, following in her older sister's footsteps. That was usually the pattern—Gabi was the little sister tagging along in her sister's sports path.

I first met Gabi in my Algebra 2 class. She was a pretty good student, but she also spent the entire hour talking to anyone who'd listen. She did all her homework at night and used the school day to socialize. It worked for her—she consistently earned A's—but it drove all of her teachers crazy. Still, she was charming and funny, and as much as I wanted her to focus more in class, I did genuinely enjoy having her there every day.

Barely over five feet tall, Gabi was athletic but undersized. When she told me she was thinking about joining the track team that spring and wanted to try high jump, I had to be honest and break down the physics for her: She was simply too short. But pole vault? I told her that might work. I loved her energy and thought she'd be a great addition to the vault squad, not just because of her athletic ability, but because of her personality.

After just one practice at Aquinas College, it was obvious: Gabi was fast and fearless, two nonnegotiables for pole vault success. And that was it—she became a vaulter. From that moment on, we spent a lot of time together. She became like family, and she quickly rose to become one of the top vaulters on our team and in the entire state of Michigan.

One day during her junior year, Gabi told me she'd be late to practice because she had to meet with a teacher. It was an odd excuse, and something didn't sit right. I followed up with the teacher—and sure enough, Gabi had lied. To be fair, she had skipped practice to console a close friend who was going through a tough time. But she had still looked me in the eye and lied.

I was crushed. I thought we had the kind of relationship where she could be honest with me about anything. If she needed a day off, especially for something like that Helping a friend, all she had to do was tell me. The next day, I suspended her for two practices and a meet. And it wasn't just any meet—it was a big one. Missing it could have hurt her chances of being recruited for college.

I knew the decision came with risk. I could've lost her trust or lost her altogether. But I believed the consequence was necessary and that our relationship was strong enough to survive it. I wasn't willing to compromise on integrity—not even for my most talented athlete. What's more, I knew this could be a defining moment for her. Whether she grew from it or walked away, she would understand that honesty matters.

A few days later, Gabi walked into my classroom, broke down in tears, and asked for forgiveness—not to get back in the lineup, just to be forgiven. She told me I was one of the only adults in her life she could rely on, and she promised she'd never lie to me again. That moment changed us both. I believed her, and I forgave her. And she never broke that trust again.

Her senior year was full of highlights: She became an All-State pole vaulter, long jumper, and relay team member. By the time we reached the national championship meet, she'd had an incredible season, but she still hadn't landed a major college offer.

Then fate stepped in.

While Gabi was competing, the University of Louisville coach, Brooke Rasnick, sat near me. I had crossed paths with Brooke a few times before. She was a tough, passionate coach and an incredible leader of athletes. Naturally, we started talking about the spark plug I was coaching.

I told her Gabi had only been vaulting a couple of years but had unbelievable potential. More importantly, I said to Brooke, she was an exceptional person. By the end of our conversation, I felt confident I had just introduced Gabi to her next coach. Brooke was the perfect fit, and I trusted her to guide Gabi on the next leg of her journey.

Gabi went on to become an NCAA champion in pole vault and a professional athlete. She's now a two-time world team member.

To this day, she still brings up the time we had that tough moment about honesty. Once, after she broke up with a boyfriend, I asked her why. He seemed like a nice kid, and I figured they had a future. She looked at me and said, "He lied to me. We don't hang out with liars."

Gabi holds herself and the people around her to a high standard of honesty, and that standard has served her well.

Integrity will always rise to the top.

Future NCAA Champion Gabi Leon! (*Photo by Jim Swoboda*)

CHAPTER 12

Bandits: You Can Only Have One

You become like the five people you spend the
most time with. Choose carefully.
—Jim Rohn

ONE OF MY favorite administrators was Dave Chesney, the assistant principal at East Kentwood Freshman Campus. His job was not an easy one, managing a building with over eight hundred freshmen. On top of that, Dave was an NCAA football official. His calm, steady temperament made him the perfect fit for both roles.

Dave was full of valuable wisdom, but one lesson has stuck with me more than any other. He used to say:

"Bandits: You can only have one per team, or they will multiply."

Dave defined a "bandit" as a kid who plays by their own rules. Bandits are often incredibly talented, but their behavior can isolate them from the rest of the team. If managed well, one bandit might not derail a program. But the moment you add a second, problems multiply. Their influence can spread quickly, creating division, distraction, and a culture that becomes harder to lead.

As a bandit myself, I understand what it's like to push back on everything and everyone. I know what it's like to think you know more than you really do. In fact, I appreciate bandits for the spice they bring. No one wants to be surrounded by a group of boring rule followers. These are the young men and women who push the limits and occasionally cross the line. Truthfully, most of the athletes highlighted in this book probably have a little bandit in them, and some of the greatest people on Earth carry that same spirit. But for a coach, they can certainly be a lot of work.

The truth is, a bandit is often a misunderstood kid coming from a tough home life. These athletes may struggle to adjust to team expectations simply because they have not lived in an environment where social norms are modeled and followed. That does not excuse their behavior, and it does not change the fact that a bandit can be extremely disruptive. But it does help us understand the "why" behind the actions and gives us a possible road map for change.

When we can trade poor decision-making for accountability and structure, we do more than help one athlete. We protect the team and create a culture where every athlete can thrive.

The key is isolation, limiting this maverick tendency to one person. A focused, disciplined team can steer a lone bandit in the right direction. But two bandits? They'll feed off each other, undermining everything you've built. But when you have a single bandit on your team—that athlete who struggles to follow rules—you can isolate and redirect their rogue attributes, recognizing that, despite their challenges, they may still bring value to the team beyond just their athletic ability.

Ask yourself the following questions:

- Are they a good kid at heart?
- Do they need the team more than the team needs them?
- Are you trying to help them grow and mature?

For whatever reason they are on the team, the single bandit will always be manageable and perhaps even useful to the process of team building. But if you have a second bandit in close proximity, things get exponentially harder.

For example, if two linemen both struggle with authority on a football team, they will reinforce each other's behavior. If you're trying to get Jimmy to show up on time, but Stevie is also late every day, your challenge more than doubles. They have support in their behavior, and now you are fighting against a broader resistant mindset, not just an individual.

On the other hand, if Jenny is zoning out during a team meeting but the rest of the locker room is engaged, you have a much better chance of isolating the issue and correcting it.

Multiple bandits feed off each other and defy focused attention from coaches trying to get them in line.

Your odds of changing behavior increase when you're dealing with just one, but they decrease dramatically when they multiply. And make no mistake: They will multiply, like gremlins. Often, bandits are exploited—and their behavior perpetuated—by previous teachers and coaches who haven't intercepted bad habits and invested in the kid's development, only using them for their raw talent. These coaches or teachers enable the behavior through inaction.

When I think of pro sports, I think of all the "bad boys" who made it big. Not all of them were successful in the long run, but as a Pistons fan, one that comes to mind is Dennis Rodman. As a kid, I loved "The Worm" and admired his success. At the height of his career, Dennis was on the Chicago Bulls. He was surrounded by structure, high-character teammates, and a coach, Phil Jackson, who provided guardrails to keep him on track.

But imagine if Dennis had been on the same team as Ron Artest or Allen Iverson, notable mavericks in the NBA. It would've been chaos. By avoiding multiple wild cards on one team, those organizations were enforcing the "Single Bandit Rule." Whether you're managing a sports team or a sales force, it's okay to have one person who thinks outside the box or pushes boundaries—but not two. Being a bandit looks like a lot of fun and can inspire innovation, but if you have two bandits, you'll have six by the end of the week.

The Bandit Rule in Action

This principle is especially critical in sports with cuts, where talent often takes precedence over culture. For example, if you've got a starter who's a bandit and a bench player who amplifies that bad behavior, one of them has to go. Whatever decision you make in this scenario, while it's tempting to choose players based purely on skill, team culture has to be the more important consideration. Culture drives success, and without it, even the most talented teams will fail. As a team ascends toward championships, the little things matter more and more. In all sports, margins shrink as the season progresses. Culture may be more intangible than individual talent on display, but it more often provides the edge that will make up for those shrinking margins.

Early in the season, when you're competing within your league, there is often a larger margin for error. Mistakes provide learning opportunities, and most won't end your season—many won't even cost you the game. However, your team's reaction to mistakes will dictate how you move forward, and this reaction is dependent on team culture.

As the season progresses, all teams improve. Every opponent has been working toward this moment, just like you. Mistakes—and the critical reactions to them—will have a greater impact on your outcomes.

Culture is how you overcome adversity. Having athletes on your team who do not buy into your team's ultimate goals and culture can wear on coaches, teammates, and other supporters of your program. While bandits can add a unique energy to the team, keeping them around certainly comes with a risk-reward proposition from the head coach.

Great coaching alone is not enough to win championships. Your team must be prepared to handle anything that happens on the field of play without direction from adults. This is where culture plays its biggest role in winning and losing. Ask yourself the following questions:

- Have you built a culture where leaders can lead?
- Does your team know how to follow when following is required?
- Do they have the authority to make important decisions without fear of retribution?
- Are they skilled enough to make the right decisions?

Bandits do not have to be bandits forever. They can become an important part of your team's fabric. Some of the greatest moments in sports—both in movies and real life—feature the bandit turned hero. But in order to do this, they need a strong, positive environment to grow. They can't thrive if they're surrounded by enablers.

Will your culture support that transformation or delay it?

This emphasis on culture doesn't just apply to athletes; it applies to parents too. If a parent undermines the team's culture, you may need to have a tough conversation with them—or, in some extreme cases, let their child go. It's never an easy decision, but sometimes it's necessary for the greater good.

The Redemption of Bandits

Every bandit needs attention, mentorship, and accountability. Without those, things often end poorly. But when a coach invests time and effort into building a relationship with them, incredible transformations can happen.

Bandits often test boundaries because of trust issues or a lack of positive role models. But when they realize a coach genuinely cares about them and their growth, they become fiercely loyal. When we invest in the athletes who need it the most, transformational coaching becomes a life-saving experience. Where else will a young person be held accountable for their actions and actually want to change their behavior?

Athletics provides the carrot—just enough incentive to make someone want to change. And that change will not be temporary, but lasting.

I am most proud of my former bandits who have gone on to do great things.

Athlete Profile: Khance Meyers, Class of 2017

Khance Meyers grew up in a busy and blended household as the youngest of thirteen kids. Seven of his siblings were the biological children of one or both parents, and five were adopted. As the baby of the family, Khance learned to stand out with a mix of charm, talent, and defiance. His relationship with his father was strained, which I could relate to in a personal and meaningful way. In fact, his dad only made it to one track meet during Khance's entire career.

From early on, it was obvious Khance had rare sprinting ability. By seventh grade, he had already fallen in love with track, and the Amateur Athletic Union (AAU) circuit helped sharpen his skills. In eighth grade, he won our Battle of the Woods meet, held between all three of our middle schools, and set the Crestwood Middle School 400-meter record. He was training nearly ten months a year before he even entered high school.

As a freshman coached by Jeff McCune, he showed flashes of brilliance but still needed time to mature. His sophomore year was promising during the indoor season, but he was academically ineligible to compete in the spring. That setback hit hard and forced him to reflect on what needed to change.

He returned his junior year with the same incredible talent and the same unpredictability. He joined the team a few days late after AAU Nationals and would often arrive after practice had already started, skipping warm-ups and following his own plan. During character talks, he was distracted and sometimes wore headphones. There was a lot of turmoil at home, and it showed. While some interpreted his behavior as arrogance, what I saw was a teenager going through a lot and not knowing how to express it.

A major source of conflict came from his offseason AAU training, which clashed with our team philosophy and structure. There were no blatant violations, just a poor attitude that affected teammates and coaches alike. Still, it didn't come from a bad place. Khance was impulsive, independent, and full of teenage angst, but his heart was good. He made plenty of mistakes but rarely repeated them. He loved the sport and wanted to be great. Helping him reach that greatness would take work.

We never gave him a free pass. If anything, we held him to higher standards. There were many frustrating moments, but we never stopped believing in who he could become. There were times I wondered if we would have fought so hard for him if he weren't so talented. Maybe not. But I also believe this: If he didn't love the sport as much as he did, he wouldn't have tolerated how hard we pushed him either. It worked because both sides stayed committed, even when it was difficult.

We used our "One Bandit Rule" to protect our culture. It was not meant to single him out. We paired him with strong leaders—not necessarily the fastest runners, but those who could keep him grounded and focused. Trust was everything. He had the speed to win, but learning to trust his teammates and coaches took time. By the end of his junior year, he was a state champion in the 100, 200, and 4×200.

He also placed second at the national championship meet with an impressive time of 20.78.

His senior year started with more tension. He missed offseason bonding and arrived a few days late to spring practice after traveling for AAU. He didn't seem fully bought in. On his first day of the season, I pulled him aside and set up a meeting with his mom. We laid out our concerns and presented a contract outlining expectations for academics, effort, behavior, and leadership. It wasn't punishment. In fact, it was a structure we all agreed to.

The meeting was tense. I told him clearly that if he didn't fully commit, the season would be lost. I knew this contract would hold him accountable but it would also force our coaching staff to hold ourselves to high standards. He was too powerful an influence not to be all in. He signed the contract, stood in front of the team, and pledged to lead. As a coach, this was a serious gamble. I was willing to lose him as a team member, but I was not willing to argue with him all season.

That spring, Khance had a season for the ages. He broke the Michigan state record in the 100 meters and won state titles in the 200, 4×200, and 4×400. He was named "Mr. Track and Field," the highest honor a high school athlete can earn in Michigan. The names on that list include NCAA champions, world medalists, and Olympians.

But it was who he became that mattered most. At one meet, I watched as Khance corrected a younger teammate for losing focus. The same kid who once ignored our talks was now giving his own. That's when I knew it had all been worth it.

We loved Khance like one of our own. We stayed close because we knew he was vulnerable, and staying involved mattered. When he finally learned to make good decisions on his own, we could breathe a little easier. Our approach in dealing with this immensely gifted bandit worked. He went on to become a National Junior College Athletic Association All-American, represented Team USA at the

U20 World Championships, and competed for a year at Kentucky, with another year at Western Carolina. Today—believe it or not—he continues to give back selflessly, coaching track at Belleville West in Illinois.

Khance's story is one of growth, redemption, and trust. It remains one of the most powerful reminders I have that coaching is never just about nurturing talent.

I think it's important to note here that I'm equally proud of Khance and Tyrone (whom I highlighted in Chapter Seven). They are redemption stories, but more than that, their experiences reflect growth in my own coaching journey. These two athletes had a lot in common. Both were the youngest children in their families, raised primarily by their mothers. Both were incredibly talented. Both had strong personalities, big egos, and their own way of doing things. As the youngest sibling in their respective families, each of them often felt they should be the center of attention.

With Tyrone, his behavior reached a point where it simply couldn't continue without severe consequences; we made the decision to dismiss him from the team during his junior year. Thankfully, it turned out to be the wake-up call he needed, and he returned for his senior season a completely different person. With Khance, we found ourselves in a similar situation, but this time, instead of suspension, we chose a different path. We invited his mother to meet with us and worked together on a contract that clearly laid out expectations and accountability.

Looking back, I wonder if Tyrone might have benefited from the same approach. Maybe a parent meeting and a structured agreement could have helped him even earlier. As coaches, we must continually grow in our craft, and growth inevitably involves the potential for mistakes. To be strong, supportive coaches, we must reflect on both the good and the bad, asking ourselves what we could have done better and striving to improve each time.

I'm thankful that Coach Frank didn't kick me off the team when I was a teenager, as I'm pretty confident I was more of a bandit than Tyrone or Khance could ever be. I have no idea where my life would have gone if he had dropped me. I'm proud of how things ended for both Khance and Tyrone, but when I look back at their stories, I also see opportunities for growth in myself. I hope and trust the next time a bandit walks into the locker room, full of teenage angst, a massive ego, and a deep love for the sport, I'll be even better prepared to help guide them through it.

CHAPTER 13

Hard Work Beats Talent When Talent Doesn't Work Hard

The only place where success comes before work is in the dictionary.
—Vidal Sassoon

AS COACHES, OUR mission is to find talent. Talent is like gold—it holds immense value for a team, and we will go to great lengths to uncover it. Talent can turn an average season into a great one, elevating a good team to championship caliber. Our school is no exception. Like every athletic program in America, our coaches constantly search for talent.

This search for talent is most apparent at two key moments in our district:

1. **When a new student moves in.** If they have any athletic experience at their previous school, coaches are eager to meet them. Could this new student possess hidden talent that surpasses the thousands of students already in our system?

We can determine this more clearly, because we've already vetted the other students when they first arrived.

2. **During fifth-grade "field day."** This two-day event at our stadium involves all ten elementary schools, each competing in a giant track meet. The format is modified to include events like the kick blast (kicking a rubber ball for distance), softball toss, horizontal jump, agility run, and traditional races like the 50m, 70m, hurdles, 200m, and 400m. The day concludes with a tug-of-war contest.

To the casual observer, this might seem like a fun school event. To a coach, it's a scouting combine. Smart coaches are out there, watching closely, handing out flyers for camps and clinics, and planting the first seeds of recruitment. This may inflate a few young egos, but even at this early stage with fifth-grade competitors, the event carries all the emotions of the Olympics—the joy of victory and the agony of defeat.

So yes, talent is important. But for every naturally gifted athlete—those who are tall, fast, or naturally strong—there are dozens of kids who weren't born with those advantages and will have to grind their way to the top.

That's why talent alone is never enough.

The Journey from Talent to Hard Work

I attend fifth-grade field day every year in the hopes of finding natural athletes, but I also recognize that talent alone won't lead to consistent success. We must build a culture of hard work and dedication. And if an exceptionally talented athlete joins our team, we need to be ready to elevate their gifts with that same work ethic.

After fifth-grade field day, as these young athletes move into middle school, they enter a world of structured, school-run athletics. Unlike rec leagues coached by parents, school sports introduce more demanding practices, competition, and accountability.

Some kids—once dominant in fifth grade—will waste their talent and get passed by their harder-working counterparts. The reasons vary:

- **Ego:** They've been told they're great for so long that they've never had to work hard. Learning this lesson late can be painful.
- **Growth and Maturity:** The oversized fifth grader might be an average-sized eighth grader. Growth spurts can cause temporary awkwardness, disrupting their coordination and performance.
- **Lack of Challenge:** If they never had to push themselves in the past, they struggle when their natural gifts no longer guarantee success.

As varsity coaches, we inherit these athletes. We unpack years of inflated egos and introduce a culture where hard work is the standard. This is why many top varsity teams implement awards like the "Hard Hat Award" or "Grinder of the Week"—reinforcing the value of effort over entitlement.

The Talent Code vs. the Sports Gene

Let me begin by saying that selling hard work to teenage boys is harder than selling a ketchup sandwich to a woman in white gloves.

I've read many books on athletic performance, always searching for ways to inspire my athletes. One book that initially shook my belief in hard work was *The Sports Gene* by David Epstein.[3] This well-researched, compelling book explores the genetic advantages of great athletes. Epstein argues that elite runners tend to come from

---

3 David Epstein, *The Sports Gene: Inside the Science of Extraordinary Athletic Performance* (Penguin, 2013).

Kenya, great basketball players are born tall, and that certain genetic traits are almost necessary for success in specific sports.

After finishing, I was depressed. Should I just dispense with the work ethic, go back to fifth-grade field day, and simply search for talent?

Then I read *The Talent Code* by Daniel Coyle.[4] The overall theme was the opposite—talent is not purely innate but developed through deep practice, motivation, and master coaching. Coyle argues that myelin, the insulation around neural pathways, builds up through repetition and focused practice, making skills more efficient over time.

Now, my trust in balance was back in my life.

Developing Hard Workers

The talented athlete who doesn't make it to the next level is a cliché for a reason. If you've ever sat through a family reunion, you've heard countless "I coulda, woulda, shoulda" stories. These individuals will tell you that if they had it to do over again, they would have chosen hard work and dedication.

The reality is that champions are wired differently; they don't rest on laurels and accept the challenge of rigorous training. As a coach, the onus is on you to search for raw talent, but once you find it, how will you ensure that this athletic gift will be fully developed through hard work?

All sports require talent, but talent alone is not enough. A successful program must create an environment where hard work is rewarded and athletes—regardless of their natural ability—are pushed to maximize their potential.

Talent might get an athlete noticed at first, but at the end of the day, hard work is what makes champions. I often remind my athletes

---

4 Daniel Coyle, *The Talent Code: Greatness Isn't Born. It's Grown. Here's How.* (Bantam Books, 2009).

that talent is only one avenue. It can take you somewhere, but it will not take you everywhere.

Talent might open a door, earn you a chance to compete, or give you an outlet for your energy. It might even introduce you to amazing mentors or help you get into a great college. But in the end, the focus and determination of your mind will have the greatest impact on your life. The way you think, the way you respond to challenges, and the discipline you apply to areas beyond sports will shape your future.

If we can help our athletes approach the rest of their lives with the same intensity, focus, and commitment they bring to their sport, then winning will become a habit—not just in athletics, but in life.

Athlete Profile: Abby Shanahan, Class of 2007

I first met Abby Shanahan in my ninth-grade math class. She was the daughter of our longtime school custodian, John Shanahan. At first glance, Abby didn't stand out as a natural athlete—she was short, not particularly fast, and didn't possess any obvious physical gifts. But what she lacked in raw talent, she made up for with an unstoppable drive.

Early in Abby's freshman year, Jodie Olmstead, a special education case manager, approached me and asked how she was doing in class. I was taken aback by the question—Abby was one of my hardest-working students. That's when Jodie shared something surprising: This was only Abby's second year in general education.

As the story goes, Abby, who at the time was a full-time special education student, had walked into the guidance office and said, "I'm done with these classes. I want to be with everyone else." By her eighth-grade year, she had transitioned into general education. It was an incredibly bold move—she had spent much of her childhood in classes that didn't specifically prepare her for the gen-ed curriculum she aimed for. Frustrated by the lack of opportunities available to special education students, Abby was determined to succeed, no matter how difficult the transition.

Jodie explained to me that it wouldn't be easy, but Abby was relentless.

Abby wasn't alone in her family when it came to learning disabilities. She had three siblings—a younger brother and sister, and an older sister—who were also in special education. Yet, despite having no formal preparation for algebra, Abby worked incredibly hard and found success. She struggled at times, but her work ethic prevailed.

Proving Everyone Wrong

That fall, Abby joined the cross-country team and did well. In class, on the other hand, our student-teacher relationship could best be described as rocky. Abby was headstrong and wanted to prove to everyone that she was independent. Within that attitude was a spark of greatness, but it needed to be guided and focused.

With maturity often comes the realization that we do not know everything. But teaching someone to fight for themselves and believe in their own strength is far more difficult than teaching them to follow instructions. Abby already came prepared to fight. My job was to help her understand when it was time to fight and when it was better to take a step back and trust the process.

In class, I constantly pushed her to do better, and she continually rose to the challenge.

At some point, Abby told me she wanted to be a pole vaulter. I wasn't sure it was the best route for her—she was already a good cross-country runner, and given her aptitude for this, I thought she should stick to distance events. But Abby thought differently. On the first day of track season, we held a 5:30 a.m. practice for the team to pole vault, and Abby was the only girl who showed up. She was determined to prove me wrong.

As she had for everything else in her life, she knew she had to make people believe in her—and that started with me. It soon became apparent that her desire to pole vault wasn't about the event itself; it was about proving that she could do it. And in the end, she convinced me.

She was an average vaulter at first, but she worked harder than anyone and improved quickly. Her family did not attend the meets, but Mrs. Olmstead was often there, cheering her on. Over the season, her team became like family.

Abby ran cross-country in the fall and track in the spring, all while earning A's and B's in her classes. Year after year, she improved, spending every available moment running, lifting, and refining her pole vault technique. By her junior year, she was one of the top vaulters in Michigan. She also qualified for the state meet in cross-country and contributed to several relay teams in track. She was the best athlete on our team, no question.

Overcoming the Yips

During her senior year, Abby suffered a pole vaulting accident. Her hand slipped off the pole mid-jump, causing it to recoil and strike her body. The incident triggered what athletes and coaches often refer to as the "yips," a mental block that prevents an athlete from executing a skill they have performed hundreds of times before.

Pole vault is an incredibly difficult and mentally demanding sport. Every jump requires the athlete to prepare both mind and body for the possibility of impact. You sprint full speed down the runway, gripping the end of a thirteen-foot flexible fiberglass pole, and launch yourself into the air while flipping upside down in hopes of clearing the bar at maximum height. There are multiple variables that must align perfectly to complete a safe jump, let alone one that produces a successful result. Nearly every part of this process goes against what the human brain is naturally wired to accept as safe.

Therefore it is no surprise that, from time to time, the brain steps in and questions the sanity of it all. The yips are common in pole vault and have even ended professional careers. Abby's experience was a powerful reminder of how fragile the balance between confidence and fear can be in this sport.

Instead of taking off on her jumps, she hesitated and ran through. For weeks, we tried everything to combat this: We shortened her approach. I stood by the pit for reassurance. As a last resort, I even made her wear a hockey helmet. Abby hated it, but I thought it was worth a try. Then, a week before the state meet, something clicked. After making a jump, she ripped off the helmet, threw it toward me, and exclaimed, "Please throw this thing away!"

Abby had done what many professional pole vaulters couldn't: She conquered the yips through sheer will.

The State Championship Moment

The state finals were held at East Kentwood that year. We knew Abby had a chance to win, but there were lingering doubts. Would she handle the pressure? Could she continue to overcome the mental struggles of the past few weeks?

That morning, we had a special surprise.

Our principal, Joe Beel, adjusted the custodial schedule so that Abby's dad, John, would be working at the meet. But instead of his usual duties, Joe assigned him a simple task: Watch your daughter compete. When John arrived and saw Abby, the emotions were overwhelming. She adored her father, and having him there was something she had never experienced before.

As a parent, it was heartwarming. As a coach, I worried—would this additional pressure of her father's presence be too much?

Before pole vaulting, Abby ran a leg on our 4×200 relay. Then, it was time for the vault. The nerves showed early—she missed her first two attempts at 10'8", a height she had cleared many times before. But, in true Abby Shanahan fashion, she locked in and dominated the competition. She went on to clear 12'2", breaking the school record and securing the state championship.

From Special Ed to College Scholar

Abby's journey is one of the most inspiring I've ever witnessed. In eighth grade, she was a struggling student in special education. By the time she graduated, she had become the following:

- A high school graduate
- A state champion pole vaulter
- A Kansas State University scholarship athlete

At K-State, Abby continued to excel academically, eventually earning a bachelor's degree in criminal justice and sociology. Today, she serves as a police officer and is a mother of two—a testament to her resilience and relentless pursuit of excellence.

Hard work truly does beat talent when talent doesn't work hard. And Abby Shanahan is proof of that.

CHAPTER 14

Confidence Comes from Competence

The man who has confidence in himself gains the confidence of others.
—Hasidic proverb

CONFIDENCE IS A superpower. It's instantly recognizable, though hard to define. Some people walk into a room, and their presence alone commands attention. They move with purpose, speak with certainty, and carry themselves in a way that makes others take notice. Nowhere is this more evident than in athletics.

Confidence vs. Competence

One of the biggest lies in sports is that confidence alone wins games. It doesn't. Hard work does. Preparation does. Experience does. Confidence without competence is nothing more than wishful thinking. "Fake it 'til you make it" might work in other aspects of life but not in athletics.

Every year, I see this at our freshman campus. Ninth-grade athletes show up for football, track, basketball—whatever sport they play—and many of them walk in with complete confidence. They believe they're elite. They've been the best on their middle school teams, their parents have told them they're great, and their friends hype them up. They've been big fish in small ponds.

And then reality hits.

They go up against varsity athletes—bigger, stronger, more experienced players—and suddenly, their confidence means nothing. When they line up for their first drill and get blown off the line, their confidence evaporates. When they take their first shot and realize the game is faster and tougher than they expected, their belief in themselves crumbles.

This is the difference between confidence built on fantasy and confidence built on reality. In today's world—where social media creates highlight reels and everyone looks like a superstar—many young athletes believe confidence is something you generate from scratch. But it's not given. It's earned.

The Reality of Confidence

True confidence is the result of preparation, repetition, and mastery. It's knowing, deep down, that you can execute, because you've done it over and over again.

A basketball player who has shot ten thousand free throws has real confidence when they step to the line. A pole vaulter who has cleared a certain height dozens of times in practice believes they can do it in competition. Their confidence isn't a guess—it's a fact. They've done the work.

One of my proudest moments as a coach was watching an athlete build confidence through competence. Years ago, we had a runner who wasn't the fastest, but he worked harder than anyone. He studied film, ran extra reps, lifted weights on his own. By his senior year, he wasn't just a leader—he was the guy everyone trusted in the biggest moments. When he stepped on the track, his confidence was real because he knew he was prepared.

The Fear of Failure

One of the biggest obstacles to confidence is the fear of failure. Athletes hesitate because they're afraid to lose, afraid to look bad, afraid to make a mistake. But when you've put in the work, failure isn't as scary.

Think about a pole vaulter. If they've consistently cleared a certain height in practice, stepping onto the runway at a big meet isn't terrifying—it's just another rep. They know they can do it. But if they haven't put in the work, that bar looks a whole lot higher.

This is why we must be honest with our athletes. We don't tell them they can't do something—we tell them they can't do it *yet*.

"Yet" is a powerful word. It shifts the mindset from impossible to eventual, as in the following examples:

- We're not at that level yet.
- We're not ready to compete with the best yet.
- We haven't developed those skills yet.

But we will eventually. And when we do, confidence won't need to be faked—it will be earned.

If you want confidence, focus on competence first. Confidence without competence is just arrogance. Genuine confidence is gained by the following:

- **Put in the work.** Show up every day, train consistently, and master the fundamentals.
- **Repetition matters.** The more you do something, the more natural it becomes.
- **Embrace failure.** Every loss and every mistake are steps toward growth.
- **Trust the process.** Don't chase confidence; chase skill, preparation, and improvement.

Remind your athletes that we don't climb the mountain in one leap. We take it one step at a time. This is the path toward building unshakable confidence—the kind that doesn't crumble under pressure, the kind that carries athletes through the biggest moments of their careers.

Athlete Profile: Kevin Jackson, Class of 2008

Kevin Jackson never won a team state title with us, but every year we win, I call him to congratulate him on another victory. He is the greatest leader I have ever coached and one of the most remarkable athletes our school has ever seen. Kevin exuded confidence—when he was in the room, there was never a question about who was in charge. As a coach, if Kevin was in your corner, his confidence poured into you. If he didn't trust you, it was easy to lose the team.

Overcoming Adversity

Kevin's childhood was anything but stable. His parents divorced when he was one, and he was raised by his mother until second grade when she became too sick to care for him. From there, he bounced around between relatives, moving from Puerto Rico to New York, changing homes every year from second to seventh grade. Eventually, he wound up with his father after seventh grade, but life remained difficult.

He lived in a trailer park with two siblings and a stepmother, and his father was incredibly tough on him—sometimes too tough.

His dad had extremely high standards. When Kevin earned a C two weeks into his freshman year, his father made him quit the football team.

After an outstanding freshman track season, Kevin decided to run cross-country as a sophomore. However, three weeks into JV basketball season that year, he was pulled from the team for talking back at home.

When Kevin wanted to join the track team as a sophomore, I insisted on meeting with his dad. I laid out clear ground rules: Kevin couldn't quit without notice, and any consequences at home couldn't spill over into the team. Surprisingly, his dad agreed.

Their relationship was complicated—his father held him to high, often unreasonable expectations and constantly reminded Kevin that he would never be as good as he supposedly was. His dad had run track in high school, but with no records to prove his performances, his stories seemed to get better every year.

Kevin wasn't chasing a friendly rivalry—he wanted to break free from the shadow his father had cast over him.

Leadership Through Sacrifice

Kevin was a state title favorite in the 400 meters, but instead of chasing individual glory, he asked to join the 4×100 relay so his teammates— particularly one senior—could qualify for the state meet with him. Initially, I declined. I explained that he was guaranteed to score points in the 400, but since the 400 and 4×100 were back-to-back races, he wouldn't be able to compete in both at full strength.

Kevin, full of confidence, said, "We'll score the same points in the 4×100 as I would in the 400, and this way, those guys can be All-State too."

Theoretically, he wasn't wrong, but the 4×100 had been inconsistent all season, and Kevin's inclusion would not necessarily change that. Unlike the 400, where we simply put our best guy on the track, the relay required three perfect baton exchanges, four flawless runs. It was risky. But Kevin was adamant.

"I'll win the 400 next year, Coach," he said.

Heading into regionals, our 4×100 had been average at best. But when Kevin joined the team, everything did change. His presence made his teammates stand taller, run faster, and believe they could win. They didn't just score points, they won. Their time of 42.20 was one of the fastest in state history.

Kevin's confidence wasn't bravado—it was built on competence. He had outworked everyone. Every rep in practice was a battle, every workout was approached with something to prove. Kevin was relentless, determined to show his father and the world that he was great.

That relay team went on to win the state championship. Kevin didn't just sacrifice for his team; he elevated them to a level they didn't even know they could reach.

Life After High School

Kevin went on to run track and play football at North Dakota State. He graduated and went on to build a life of his own. He now has two amazing children.

For years, Kevin didn't speak to his father. This past year, he has begun rebuilding that relationship, though the dynamic has shifted: Kevin is now more of the parent in their conversations. While he has limited contact with his father, which may be the healthiest choice for him, as a father, I find it incredibly sad.

But Kevin's story isn't about sadness—it's about triumph. He took the pain, the doubt, and the pressure and turned it into something remarkable. And every year, when we win another championship, I remind him: He's still a part of every victory.

Kevin receiving the baton from Zeke Crossley (Photo by Jim Swoboda)

CHAPTER 15

Tuebor

What you do today can improve all your tomorrows.
—Ralph Marston

IN 2009, THE East Kentwood track team was invited to the Michigan state capitol building to be honored by the state legislature. This recognition celebrated our historic feat: scoring seventy-nine points and being the first team from the Grand Rapids area to win the Division I state title. It was an extraordinary day for our athletes and coaches. We loaded a school bus with thirty athletes and made our way to Lansing, where we were presented with a document recognizing our achievements and given a guided tour of the capitol building.

This all took place about a month after our victory. While the team was still reveling in the glory, I was already starting to think about the next season. How could we get excited to do it all over again? That question lingered until, during the tour, a guide explained the Michigan state flag. They described how every element of the flag held meaning, and then they pointed to a Latin word: *tuebor.*

Someone asked, "What does that mean?" The guide explained, "It's Latin and translates to 'I will defend.'" Immediately, every kid on the team turned to look at me. At that moment, we became *tuebor*. We weren't just going to compete; we were going to defend what we had earned.

A Mantra Takes Shape

That year, we adopted *tuebor* as our mantra. It wasn't just about defending our state title—it was about defending our school, our teammates, and our values. Whether it was standing up for each other in the hallways or representing East Kentwood with pride on the track, *tuebor* became our guiding principle. It wasn't just a motto; it defined who we were as a team and as individuals.

In 2010, the team was on a mission. The athletes embraced the challenge, constantly asking themselves the following:

- What am I willing to defend?
- What am I willing to let go?

These questions forced everyone to reflect on what truly mattered.

When you know who you are and what you stand for, everything else becomes clearer.

Developing a Message That Matters

When developing a team message, coaches have many different avenues to explore. One of our key strategies is to hold offseason leadership meetings.

Before the season begins, we announce a preliminary meeting with the following simple announcement: "Anyone who will lead on our team this year, please meet after school."

This invitation isn't limiting—it's open to anyone who wants to step up and have a voice. At these meetings, I bring up ideas for the upcoming season, and the athletes share their thoughts as well.

Together, we ask the following questions:

- What do we think is important this year?
- What are we willing to stand for, fight against, and accept?

By the end of the meeting, we've narrowed down a few possible themes for the season. Sometimes, I feel strongly about a particular idea and push for it. Other times, the athletes rally around something else—and I let them take ownership of it. Once we finalize our theme and the athletes have bought in, we are ready to live it out throughout the season. A theme isn't just a slogan—it's an identity.

The Season of Tuebor

The 2010 team believed they could be even better than their record-breaking season the year before. They were determined to achieve something rare in track and field: back-to-back state championships. That determination fueled an unforgettable season.

At the state meet, we scored an incredible ninety-two points, winning individual titles in the 100m, 200m, 800m, 4×100 relay, and 4×200 relay. We placed in twelve of seventeen events, a display of dominance that set a new standard in Michigan track and field.

A few weeks later, we won the New Balance Nationals meet—an even greater accomplishment considering we could only compete with our senior athletes, since Michigan doesn't allow underclassmen to score at national events.

Shortly after, Nike named us the number one high school men's track team in the country and flew our seniors to Oregon for an elite competition. For many of our kids, the trip to the West Coast was their first time flying—and they flew first class, courtesy of Nike. Several athletes did not have driver's licenses and needed alternative forms of identification in order to fly.

While we didn't have our full roster in Oregon due to missing underclassmen, the experience was unforgettable. Our entire coaching staff traveled with the team, and we were about to compete at Hayward Field on University of Oregon's campus—the mecca of track and field in the United States.

Throughout the trip, we often sat together, laughing, reflecting, and marveling at how this "silly little sport" had brought us across the country. We were in awe of the incredible kids we had the privilege of coaching, knowing this was a journey they would never forget.

Nike's meet management team treated our athletes like royalty. They received free shoes, top-tier gear, unlimited food, and even a massive dance party—all first-class, all the way.

Through it all, *tuebor* remained our unifying theme. It wasn't just about defending titles—it was about defending relationships, values, and pride. The bonds formed during that season have lasted a lifetime, and the lessons learned on the track continue to shape the lives of everyone involved.

Athlete Profile: Dallas Wade, Class of 2010

Dallas Wade was an integral part of the *tuebor* season. Raised by his mother after his parents divorced, Dallas spent more time at school than anyone, whether students or staff. A true gym rat, he often trained alone, even on Sundays, secretly running stadium steps until exhaustion. We had no idea he was putting in this extra work, but it spoke volumes about his dedication and discipline.

Throughout his high school career while being coached primarily by Jeff McCune, Dallas earned nine All-State honors in both individual and relay events. But beyond his athletic accomplishments, Dallas was a truly unique individual, someone whose mind worked differently than most.

Early in his education, Dallas was placed in special education courses due to a misdiagnosis of learning disabilities. However, as he progressed, it became clear that his intelligence wasn't lacking—it was simply exceptional in different ways. Looking back, I suspect that, if it were now, he might have been diagnosed somewhere on the autism spectrum, but regardless of this, to us, Dallas was just Dallas. No labels needed.

One of his greatest gifts was for mathematics. When his teachers recognized his talent, I requested to have him in my Algebra 2 class. It was in that classroom that I saw firsthand how brilliant he truly was. At first, some classmates mistook his quiet, unique personality for a lack of intelligence. But that quickly changed when he began answering questions no one else could. For me, it was priceless watching the other students' faces as they realized Dallas was the smartest person in the room.

As a teammate, Dallas was fiercely loyal. Once you were his friend, you were a friend for life. Fortunately for us, he influenced many of his friends to join the track team.

What made Dallas special was his ability to connect with anyone. Whether you were a big, strong football player or a quiet, skinny kid from the band, Dallas treated everyone with the same level of respect and kindness. He couldn't stand conflict and worked hard to support those around him, always lifting others up.

After high school, Dallas spent a few years competing in college track but eventually realized school wasn't for him. Instead, he moved to Los Angeles to pursue a career in modeling and social media.

Dallas found success in L.A., but as always, it wasn't just about him. True to his nature, he brought several more EK kids out to L.A., helping them break into the business and guiding them along the way. Typical Dallas—always giving to others. Dallas has a way of figuring out life's equations, no matter how many variables are involved. He won't be outworked, and I have no doubt he'll continue to succeed—on his own terms.

Dallas getting ready (Photo by Jim Swoboda)

CHAPTER 16

Have a Plan and Work the Plan

The difference between successful people and really successful people is that really successful people say no to almost everything.
—Warren Buffett

THE ART OF athletics has always fascinated me. Throughout my life as both an athlete and a coach, I've been amazed at how many different ways coaches and athletes find success. No matter the sport, there are countless methods, strategies, training plans, and organizational approaches that teams use to achieve their goals.

Take football, for example. One year, a team wins the Super Bowl with a West Coast offense, and suddenly, everyone is trying to replicate it. The next year, a spread offense dominates, and the trend shifts again. In high school, you'll see teams that never throw the ball, running the Wing-T, while others pass 80 percent of the time.

Track and field is no different. I've attended countless clinics and conferences where I've heard coaches preach every philosophy imaginable. Some swear by short, high-intensity workouts, while others push for longer, lower-intensity training. Early in my coaching career,

I would latch onto the latest trends, only to find them replaced by a new "best" method the following year.

Eventually, I realized that success isn't about following the latest trend; it's about consistency. The most important thing is to have a philosophy that your team believes in. If your athletes buy in, your system—whatever it is—has a chance to work.

At the end of the day, 90 percent of every system relies on the same fundamental principles. In football, for example, you might be a running team, and I might throw the ball all game, but strong offensive line play is critical for both of us. No matter the sport, success depends on coaches and athletes preparing, executing, and understanding their roles. The details may vary, but the core of every successful program is remarkably similar.

Math, History, and Science Coaches

A few years ago, I had a late-night conversation at a track clinic with Michigan distance coach Brian Salyers from Milford High School, one of the top distance coaches in the country. We talked about coaching styles and how different coaches tend to fall into a few distinct categories.

Brian, a history teacher, called himself a "history coach." For him, everything was about themes, narratives, and motivation. He inspired his athletes with speeches about legendary competitors and historical moments. His coaching was about heart, grit, and getting his runners to believe they were fighting for something bigger than themselves.

I, on the other hand, am a math teacher—and a "math coach." I break races down into numbers. I analyze splits, track progression, and build formulas to determine the probability of success. When my predictions are right, I feel like a genius. When I'm wrong, I go straight back to the numbers to figure out what went wrong.

Then there are the "science coaches." These coaches focus on physiology—nutrition, sleep, biomechanics, and data-driven training methods. They know everything about VO_2 max, lactate thresholds, and recovery cycles. They tweak workouts down to the smallest detail to maximize performance while minimizing injury risk.

Great coaches can come from any of these categories. But to be a truly elite coach, you have to understand elements of all three. I lean heavily into the math approach, but I know that if I want to inspire my athletes, I need to deliver a powerful locker room speech now and then. I also know that ignoring nutrition completely would be a mistake.

While each coach may have a singular approach, the best coaching *staffs* are diverse in philosophy. Over the years, I've worked alongside some incredible coaches who pushed our teams in different ways. Our distance coach, Tim Gumz, is a history coach. He tells legendary stories, fires up the team, and pushes toughness over numbers. Our hurdle coach, Stephanie Stephenson, one of the best in the country, was a science teacher before she retired and moved to athletics. She's the first to notice if an athlete has a nutrition issue, and she constantly brings up recovery, injury prevention, and biomechanics.

During our peak years, our sprint coach, Jeff McCune, was both a science teacher and a bit of a math coach. He understood the physics of sprinting and had charts for everything—acceleration rates, reaction times, and projected split times for every possible scenario. Together, we made a great team. Alone, none of us would have achieved the level of success we did.

So, what kind of coach are you? Math? History? Science? Or something else entirely? Have you built a staff that complements your strengths and fills in your weaknesses?

Most new coaches start by copying someone else's model. But over time, you develop your own philosophy—the one that matches your personality and gets your athletes to believe. And that belief is what matters most.

90 Percent of Work Is Just Work

I often ask coaches if they've ever attended a clinic and felt like they knew more than the speaker. Early in my career, I would have this experience more times than I'd like to admit. Eventually, I realized a simple truth:

The event organizers asked that coach to speak—not me. Why? Probably because they had won, and I hadn't.

Usually, these coaches had just come off a state title or coached a national champion. They stood at the front of the room with credibility while I, an arrogant young coach in the audience, silently questioned their methods. And inevitably, there's always someone like I was in the crowd who raises their hand and says something like, "I don't understand why you did X. I do Y instead." This is the worst kind of audience member: one who's more interested in advertising what they know than learning something new.

The reality? That coach wasn't asked to speak because of one particular training method. They were asked because their athletes bought in, and they won. Here's the truth: **90 percent of what makes any program successful is buy-in.**

Every coach is pushing their athletes to do hard work. The determining factor isn't *what* you're doing; it's whether you can get kids to believe in it and commit to it. If you can, your program will be 90 percent as good as the best in the world.

The 10 Percent That Separates the Best

That remaining 10 percent is where championships are won. It's the expertise, the science-backed innovations, and the edge a coach brings. But that edge is not dependent on any one sure-fire innovation; go to any coaching clinic in any sport, and you'll find a coach presenting an outdated system who still wins. Why? Because, again, their athletes believe in what they're doing.

Young coaches struggle most with understanding how much work to prescribe. My advice? Just do the work and find out through that process. Training hours cannot be substituted. Look around at successful programs and learn from them. Find out what's too much or too little as you go. Young coaches often train with their athletes, which can be helpful at first in gauging intensity. I did this in my early years—until one day, age caught up with me, and I had to cut a workout short because I couldn't finish it myself. That was my last day training with my team.

Young coaches have energy and enthusiasm but lack experience. Older coaches have experience but sometimes lose the excitement and "cool factor" younger coaches bring. The key is balance—pushing hard enough to get results without breaking your athletes physically or mentally.

Most revolutionary training methods start with a coach who has a new idea and, most importantly, a group of athletes willing to buy in. Years later, a scientist comes along and validates the idea's efficacy with research. The coach didn't do research; they had a hunch from experience, or they simply thought of something that appealed to their particular coaching style. Either way, the buy-in by the team and the training hours to test the idea were indispensable. Because 90 percent of work is just work. The other 10 percent is the expertise gained through experience and the art of coaching that emerges from that expertise—this is where your philosophy comes in.

Find what works for you. Build a philosophy that fits your personality.

Athlete Profile: Ricco Hall, Class of 2011

In 2010, East Kentwood won everything there was to win. We were on top of the world, scoring ninety-two points at the state meet—a record that still stands. But the following year, we returned zero athletes who had scored at that meet. It was going to be a struggle, to say the least.

That fall, a new family moved into our district, with two children entering EK: twins Rebecca and Ricco Hall. As the largest and most diverse school in Michigan, we see a lot of athletes move in and out, newly joining our teams as sophomores, juniors, or seniors. Ricco joined the boys' team that spring as a senior, but his first three years in track and field at another school had been unremarkable. At first glance, when he arrived, he seemed like just another average athlete.

But that first impression didn't last long.

Unlocking Potential

It didn't take us long to realize that Ricco was something special—he just didn't know it yet. He had never been part of a structured training program, and his raw talent had carried him through previous competitions. Once he started following a real training regimen, his improvement was immediate and dramatic.

Ricco moved to East Kentwood in early November and began training with us twice a week right away. By winter, he was making small but steady improvements. His form was sharper, his conditioning was improving, and he started attending indoor meets.

For a sprinter, indoor track is much tougher than outdoor—tighter corners, different surfaces, and a heavier emphasis on strength over pure speed. Yet by the end of the indoor season, Ricco had already broken his outdoor personal best in the 400. That was the first sign that something big was coming.

When outdoor season began, his progress accelerated. With the expertise of our sprint coach, Jeff McCune, Ricco refined his technique, sharpened his mechanics, and continued to improve.

Week after week, Ricco got faster.

He had run 11.0 seconds in the 100-meter dash the previous season. By midseason, he was a 10.9 guy. Then 10.8. And he was undefeated. That's when we realized that Ricco's only competition was himself.

At his old school, he had been so dominant that his times were dictated by how fast he needed to go to win—not how fast he was actually capable of running. If he was winning comfortably, he wouldn't push to his limits. We had to break that mentality. The goal wasn't just to win races—it was to run as fast as possible. By the time of the state meet, Ricco was ready.

The State Meet

Ricco's state meet performance was legendary. He won four state titles that day:

- 100 meters—state record, 10.55
- 400 meters—state record, 47.0
- 4×200 relay—state meet record, 1:26.34
- 4×400 relay—3:19.95, beating the next team by 2.5 seconds

By the time the 4×400 relay arrived, Ricco was exhausted. He had already run a 100-meter prelim, a semifinal, and the final where he broke the state record. Then he ran on the record-setting 4×200 relay. Finally, with almost no rest, he shattered the 400-meter state record.

By the 4×400, he had nothing left.

We knew it, and his teammates knew it. So, before the race, we put the pressure on our three other relay members who would precede Ricco's anchor leg. We told them, "Give Ricco a huge lead. He'll get us across the line, but he can't do this alone."

They delivered.

By the time Ricco grabbed the baton, our lead was over twenty meters. He cruised to victory, securing one of the greatest individual performances in Michigan high school track history.

Ricco was named Michigan's "Mr. Track & Field," awarded to the best male track athlete in the state across all divisions. That day, Nebraska track coach Billy Maxwell came to watch Ricco. He had planned to offer him a small scholarship, unsure of what to expect. After seeing Ricco's record-breaking 400 meters, he stood up and said, "Coach, I've got to go. I came with an offer I can't present anymore. Let Ricco's mom know I'll offer him a full-ride scholarship." Billy didn't even stay for the rest of the meet.

Ricco would eventually receive offers from schools all over the country, but he stayed loyal to that first offer from Nebraska and Coach Maxwell. Weeks before the state meet, we had called countless college coaches, trying to get someone to pay attention. Nobody returned our calls.

Billy did, and Ricco repaid that belief by becoming an NCAA All-American.

The 90 Percent Meets the 10 Percent

Ricco Hall is what happens when the 90 percent meets the 10 percent—when natural talent gets turbocharged with coaching, training, and belief.

If you get 100 percent of your athletes to complete a training program that's 90 percent effective, you will beat every coach who has a 100 percent effective program that only gets 75 percent buy-in. In the end, belief matters more than any training system. Ricco went from an average high school sprinter to one of the best in Michigan history. And all it took was the right training, the right coaching, and a relentless work ethic.

CHAPTER 17

Chocolate Chip Cookies

*Excellence is in the details. Give attention to
the details and excellence will come.*
—Perry Paxton

I LOVE CHOCOLATE CHIP cookies. In my opinion, they are the best cookies ever invented. Over the years, I've been fortunate to try many versions of this supreme cookie from different bakers, bakeries, and even students' parents. When I was a young teacher and coach, I made sure everyone knew how much I loved them. This wasn't just a fun fact I shared about myself; it was a strategic move. I figured if my students and athletes knew, maybe—just maybe—I'd get a batch now and then. It worked; I've had some incredible cookies over the years. And, of course, I've had to fake my way through a few bad ones, smiling politely while chewing my way through something barely edible.

Now that I'm older, I try to avoid them in excess, but their allure remains irresistible. At least once a year, I use cookies to make a point to my team. "Who loves cookies?" I ask. It's an easy question to ask a group of teenage boys, followed by "What's the best cookie?" I let them debate the question for a few minutes before unilaterally settling it: "The chocolate chip cookie."

A chocolate chip cookie consists of a few basic ingredients—flour, sugar, eggs, butter, and chocolate chips. Good cookies and bad cookies share these same core components. Yet, even with the same ingredients, some cookies turn out amazing while others completely miss the mark. A recipe is printed right on the back of the chocolate chip bag—hard to mess up, right? Yet, in spite of this, I've eaten my fair share of bad ones. So, what makes the difference? Timing. Preparation. Precision.

Lessons from Cookies

The care taken to produce a perfect chocolate chip cookie is actually an excellent analogy for the care required to be an effective coach.

Timing Matters

Preheating the oven to 375 degrees Fahrenheit takes patience. In fact, it often takes longer than mixing the ingredients. Baking time ranges from nine to eleven minutes, depending on the oven—a seemingly small detail, but an important one. Do you have a nine-minute oven or an eleven-minute oven? Do you prefer your cookies soft or slightly firmer? Experience teaches these nuances.

In life, just like in baking, timing is everything. Whether it's peaking at the right time in a season, making a key adjustment in training, or knowing when to rest, the details matter.

Preparation Is Key

Softened butter is essential. But how softened? If you pull it straight from the fridge, it's too hard. If you wait too long, it melts, and your dough loses structure. If you microwave it, you risk uneven consistency—half liquid, half solid. Every baker knows that skipping proper preparation affects the final product.

The same is true in athletics. Some teams enter a season without a real preseason conditioning plan. There are many teams that do this. But how many great teams do? Very few. Preparation—whether in training, recruiting, or strategizing—directly impacts results. If you want success, you have to plan for it.

The Right Ingredients and Extras

Every recipe has room for personal flair. Vanilla extract, brown sugar, or even nuts can enhance a chocolate chip cookie. But pile on too many extras, and you ruin the balance. A cookie with butterscotch, cranberries, and coconut might sound creative, but is it actually good? Probably not.

Teams are no different. The foundation—effort, discipline, teamwork—must always be there. But what about the extras? Does your team have the right mix of athletes? Does the coach need to recruit in the hallways or pull in multi-sport athletes to fill key roles? The best teams don't just show up—they're built, one ingredient at a time.

Baking and Building a Team

No baker sets out to make a bad cookie, just as no coach or athlete sets out to fail. But without thought, care, and attention to detail, success becomes far less likely. Imagine going into a season with no plan—no strategy for conditioning, no lineup adjustments, no game plan. How would you even know if you're heading in the right direction?

Great teams don't just happen. They require planning, patience, and precision. The best cookies aren't made on the first try, and the worst cookies aren't baked after years of experience. Success, whether in the kitchen or on the field, is all about preparation, execution, and the willingness to learn from each batch. How will you approach your next batch of cookies?

Athlete Profile: Nolan Meister, Class of 2016

Nolan Meister was born into one of the most loving homes you can imagine. His mother, an elementary schoolteacher, and his father, an engineer, created an environment filled with support and encouragement. Win, lose, or draw, Nolan was loved unconditionally. In all the years I coached him, I never once heard his parents speak critically of him. Nolan's life was free from adverse childhood experiences, a rare and powerful gift. But what set Nolan apart was not his circumstances. It was how he chose to use them.

As a freshman, Nolan focused on two things: school and running. He was an above-average distance runner—coached by Tim Gumz—who fully embraced the process. He believed running was the ultimate meritocracy. The more effort you put in, the more success you earned. In the classroom, Nolan was exceptional. He took precalculus as a ninth grader and often tutored older teammates who struggled more than he did. By the time he graduated, Nolan had earned more than fifty college credits through dual enrollment. He was a National Merit Scholar, held the highest GPA in our school, and never missed an assignment. He earned a full-ride scholarship to the University of Oklahoma to study meteorology, a dream he had nurtured since second grade.

Unlike many athletes who are driven by external pressure, Nolan was different. He ran simply for the love of testing his limits. His growth mindset made a lasting impact not only on himself but also on those around him. He cared deeply about the team, and no one was prouder to lift a state championship trophy than Nolan. Certainly, no one deserved it more.

When Nolan joined our program in 2013, our distance group was not particularly strong. His steady leadership helped change that. One of my favorite stories came during his junior year. Just days before the season started in early March, Nolan had surgery to repair a torn meniscus. I was surprised to see him show up on crutches the first day of practice. I assumed his season was over and said, "We'll get you ready for cross-country." Nolan looked at me and replied, "I'll see you at the state finals." He spent the season recovering and cross-training, and by the end of the year, he had qualified for yet another state final. In the end, Nolan competed at every state meet in both cross-country and track from his sophomore through senior year.

On the track and in the classroom, Nolan was dependable, focused, and consistent. He never quite reached All-State status as an individual, but he was the backbone of our team. He had a strong sense of what the team needed and always showed up with the right attitude. He was thoughtful, internally motivated, and a joy to coach.

Nolan often says the most important lessons he learned in high school came from the leadership opportunities he found through track and cross-country. After graduation, he stepped away from competitive running, satisfied with what he had accomplished. He went on to earn his meteorology degree from the University of Oklahoma and now works for the National Weather Service in Norman, Oklahoma.

Nolan Meister is the kind of person who leads with patience, precision, and purpose. He represents everything that is right about high school athletics. I am incredibly proud of the man he has become. Nolan understands what it takes to succeed, just like baking the perfect chocolate chip cookie: You need timing, patience, and a great plan.

CHAPTER 18

It Sucks to Suck

You may have to fight a battle more than once to win it.
—Margaret Thatcher

WHEN WE DISCUSS work ethic and effort with kids, we often fall back on the following quip: "It sucks to suck." This isn't meant to be insulting but rather to show empathy and let them know we understand how they're feeling. It's not fun to work so hard at something and not see growth or success. No one wants to be on a losing team or fail to improve. However, the reality is that winning is hard. If it were easy, everyone would do it. Both sides in any competition want to win, and both have worked hard—yet only one can prevail.

It truly does suck to suck. No one likes that feeling. But when you're striving for greatness, the pain of losing often becomes a more powerful motivator than the joy of victory. After a tough loss, athletes will hear countless voices telling them to "shake it off" or "move on." While this is well-intentioned and potentially helpful, I also make sure to remind them, "Never forget this feeling."

This feeling will be what drives them to get up for optional workouts, finish one more rep, or skip the Saturday night party to get the rest they need. "It sucks to suck" isn't a permanent state; it's a choice. Losing is painful, but it's also controllable. Winning championships requires confronting that pain head-on, not running from it.

We see this dynamic most clearly in AAU or club competitions, where athletes compete multiple times in a weekend. Winning and losing become routine, and the emotional highs and lows are muted. Athletes often run from the feeling of failure, but they should embrace it. This doesn't mean spiraling into despair over every loss but rather learning to compartmentalize those emotions and use them as motivation.

While it's important to recognize the feeling of failure, it's also important to not fixate on it for too long. We generally give athletes five to ten minutes to feel upset after a loss. After that, it's time to process, find the lesson, and move forward. Reflecting on failure helps athletes make the adjustments needed for future success. Blowing off a loss or sinking into deep depression isn't helpful. Instead, athletes need to find the positives in every performance, even those that don't go as planned. Otherwise, the same patterns will repeat.

Winning is never guaranteed, but growth is always an option. Every setback is an opportunity to learn. Growth isn't linear—it's two steps forward and one step back. After every fall, there's a chance to grow stronger. Calluses, both physical and emotional, are formed through challenges and struggles. And calluses are always tougher than soft skin.

Athlete Profile: Colton Emeott, Class of 2020

Colton is my oldest son. When he was young, I'm not sure we ever thought he'd develop into an athlete, but we knew he loved to compete. He took losses hard, and we spent a lot of time discussing how to work through those tough moments. Like all of our kids, Colton tried every sport: tennis, golf, football, track, soccer, basketball, and baseball.

One particular day stands out from Colton's Little League baseball days. I had come from track practice to watch him play. As a track coach with a lot of time-consuming obligations, I hadn't made it to many baseball games, so I was excited to watch. I sat next to some other dads I didn't know as Colton stepped up to bat. He hit the ball to third base, which in that league was usually an automatic single—kids typically struggled to field, throw, and catch the ball in time. However, on this day, after several bobbles and a weak throw to first base, Colton was still thrown out by a mile.

The dads next to me joked, "Hey, that's the track coach's kid!" It was funny until I realized my wife had also heard them, and then I took it more personally. Colton was the slowest kid on the team while I coached some of the fastest kids in the country. That evening, I started speed and agility training with Colton in our backyard. But I quickly realized he wasn't interested in listening to his dad. So, the following week, I started a speed and agility program for young kids in our district, thinking that others his age could potentially influence him. Positive peer pressure was exactly what Colton needed. That first week, we had almost 200 young kids show up for our first youth Speed and Agility session.

Over the years, we invested in travel baseball, which we thought was the right path for him. He had an amazing coach, Dave Coble, who mentored him, and we were thrilled. But at the end of his seventh-grade season, Colton announced he'd played his last baseball game and wanted to join the track team.

I didn't see it coming, and I wasn't sure how successful he'd be. But Colton embraced "the suck" more than anyone I've ever seen. That same slow kid from little league baseball had become a bonafide track star. He took losses hard but always found the positives and implemented the lessons he learned. As a pole vaulter, he earned the nickname "PV Brat" for his temper tantrums after failed competitions. It was embarrassing for me as his dad, but I didn't want to squash his passion. Over time, and after many conversations, he learned to channel his emotions constructively.

Colton developed quickly as a pole vaulter and long jumper (coached in the latter by Matt Burton), and he eventually earned a scholarship to the University of Nebraska. However, his senior year of high school was derailed by COVID-19, and his first two years in college brought coaching changes and other setbacks. For three years, Colton saw no improvements in his personal records.

But he never gave up. He once again embraced the suck and transferred to Grand Valley State University to be closer to home. During his junior year, he finally had a breakthrough. As a member of the GVSU track and field team, he became a multiple-time conference champion and qualified for the national championships four times. He reached a personal record of 16'8", and we could not be more proud of his dedication to the sport.

As I write this, Colton has completed his collegiate pole-vaulting career and is now focused on becoming a high school science teacher and track coach. I am extremely proud of the man he has become.

Living in "the suck" for years finally paid off. Colton's perseverance and his ability to absorb failure and move forward are what truly set him apart.

Colton up and over (Photo by Jim Swoboda)

CHAPTER 19

Locker Room Speech: The SLANT Method

Success is nothing more than a few simple disciplines, practiced every day.
—Jim Rohn

When I was in my freshman year of college at Saginaw Valley State University, our team was struggling academically, and I might have been part of the problem. I was a horrible student. If there were a poster child for poor academics, it would have been me. I sat in the back of the class. I slept frequently. I never took notes. I had horrible relationships with professors. You name the bad habit, I had it. Finally, one day, Coach Jim Nesbitt gave us a playbook—not for football, but for how to be a student.

It wasn't the usual "Do your homework and study hard" speech. This was different. What I didn't realize at the time was that being a student was just like every sport I had ever played. There were rules.

There was etiquette. And if you played by those rules and followed proper etiquette, school was actually an easy game.

In fact, school is much easier than sports. In sports, only one team can win. In school, theoretically, every student can earn an A. My performance in class has no impact on my neighbor's success.

On this day, Coach Nesbitt introduced us to the SLANT method. While this method wouldn't be popularized by Doug Lemov until 2010, this was only 1992. I can't tell you where Coach got it from, but he was ahead of his time. I deliver his same speech to my athletes every year. Here it is:

"Listen up! I'm about to give you a foolproof way to get better grades. Some of you are struggling, but this will help *all* of you. Even if your grades are fine, I still want you to pay attention—because this method will help you in life. It can even help when dating! And the best part? This strategy requires no extra studying, no extra time. Just effort."

SLANT

S: Sit up straight.

"Everyone, sit up nice and tall!"

Nobody likes a sloucher. Sitting up straight makes you look taller, but more importantly, it shows respect and attentiveness. Teachers appreciate it. Employers notice it. And trust me, if you're on a date, sitting up straight is a whole lot better than looking like a lifeless pile of laundry slumped in a chair.

L: Lean in.

When the teacher starts speaking, lean forward slightly. It shows you're engaged. Body language matters. It works in the classroom. It works in a job interview. And yes, it works on dates too. People want to feel like you care about what they're saying.

A: Ask one question every day.

I always remind my athletes—this is for the classroom, not for me. With 170 kids on the team, I don't need *more* questions. Save those for my assistant coaches. But in class, asking a question shows the teacher that you care. When parent-teacher conferences come around and your parents ask, "Does my child participate?" the answer will inevitably be, "Yes, every day." Teachers love that. And on a date? The ability to ask a good question can make all the difference.

N: Nod your head.

"Everyone, nod your head!"

Body language again! If you nod while the teacher talks, they'll naturally assume you're engaged. By the way, if you're on a first date and you're not nodding when the other person talks? You're probably not getting a second date.

T: Track the speaker.

Always keep your eyes on the person speaking. I walk around the room during this part of the presentation, making sure every athlete follows me with their eyes. In class, if the teacher moves, your eyes should move with them. It's a simple way to show interest and respect. And when I'm on a date, I make sure to sit where I can see both the front door and the bathroom. If my date leaves to use the restroom, I make sure to catch her eye when she comes back. Small things like this make a difference.

SLANT is a simple but effective way to become a better student, a better communicator, and a better competitor. If I can get my team—10 percent of the school—to behave this way in class, it's impossible *not* to be great.

The best part? SLANT puts you in the best position to succeed. In sports, in school, in your career, and yes—even on dates. These techniques might seem basic, but I promise you, most teenagers don't naturally do them. That's why they need to be coached.

Athlete Profile: Andre Pimpleton, Class of 2022

On our 2021 team, Andre was a junior. His journey with us was a roller coaster.

As a freshman, Andre had spent several weeks suspended for academic performance. Our policy was clear: If an athlete failed more than one class in a given week, they sat out until their grades improved. Andre was ineligible multiple times that year, though he still managed to compete in a few meets.

As a sophomore in March 2020, things unraveled further. On the first day of practice, while the rest of the team warmed up, I pulled a small group aside to inform them they were academically ineligible. No surprise, Andre was among them—he had failed two courses the previous semester and couldn't join the team.

I never dismissed kids without a word. I always spent five to ten minutes reminding them why school mattered, giving them advice, and letting them know the door was open for next year. That day, I also gave a quick refresher on the SLANT method, encouraging them to apply it in class. It wasn't personal—it was policy.

At the time, Andre was known as a student who didn't care about school. No one was surprised he was ineligible. But what did surprise me was how hard he took it. Almost to prove the point, he hadn't realized how bad his grades were until I showed him. He asked me several times if I was sure, and I even double-checked the records. The rules were the rules—he was off the team. With tears in his eyes, he nodded and walked out. Just three days later, the COVID-19 pandemic shut everything down, so technically he didn't miss more than anyone else. Still, that conversation stuck with him.

A year later, Andre returned. He was as fast as ever and trained well under our sprint coach, Jeff McCune. I honestly hadn't counted on Andre coming back, even though I'd heard he had been working hard in the offseason. When the eligibility list came out, I braced myself to see his name flagged for academic performance again—but it wasn't there. Convinced it was a mistake, I checked with our athletic director, Blaine Brumels. To our shock, Andre's grades from the first semester were all A's. His current grades? Also all A's. I had written him off too soon.

Still stunned, I asked him before practice how he'd turned things around. He said, "I remembered what you told me last year—I needed to act like I cared about class if I wanted the teachers to care about me." Andre had fully embraced the SLANT method, committing not just to his teachers but to his education as a whole.

That day, I asked him to address the team. I didn't explain why; I just said, "I want someone to talk to you about school and how to earn great grades." When Andre stood up, some kids laughed. Given his past, they assumed it was a joke. But as he walked to the front, I read off his grades—straight A's. The laughter stopped. The room of 160 boys sat up straight and listened.

Andre told them how he sat in the front row, asked to be moved away from his friends, completed every assignment, stayed awake in class, and asked questions every day—all so he'd never miss another meet. When he finished, the team applauded. I also noticed a few uncomfortable faces—kids who thought they were smarter than Andre but whose grades didn't show it.

From that moment on, Andre became a model student-athlete. He never missed another meet due to academics and became an inspiration to the team. His junior year, our weekly eligibility list was shorter than ever—our team grades had never been better.

The experience proved something I've always believed: a player-led team will always beat a coach-led team—even in the classroom.

CHAPTER 20

Feedback: The Breakfast of Champions

We all need people who will give us feedback. That's how we improve.
—Bill Gates

FROM MY VERY first year as a young teacher, I started asking my students to evaluate me. I picked this up from my college professors, who had a similar process. On the last day of class, I asked students to fill out a handwritten, anonymous survey. The questions were simple:

- Rate your overall experience on a 1–5 scale.
- What did you like?
- What could I do better?

I've always considered myself a criticism junkie. I thrive on feedback—maybe because I grew up in a tough environment where negative feedback was never in short supply. But reading these surveys was never easy.

Generally, I'd wait a few weeks after the semester ended, grab a few beers, and find a quiet place to read through them. The ratings were usually okay, and the positive comments were nice to hear. But I really focused on the criticism, looking for patterns. How many students thought I was too sarcastic? Were my tests too long? Did they think I was too harsh?

I wanted to know what they really thought, because at the end of the day, they were the ones experiencing my class. As teachers, we were evaluated by our principals, but that usually meant a few classroom visits a year—not enough to provide real insight. Occasionally, a principal would hear a complaint from a parent or student, but they rarely had a true feel for what was happening day to day.

The truth? When I was a young teacher and coach, I was growing and improving my pedagogy every day. At times, I could be a bully. I raised my voice, flexed my authority, and manipulated kids to get what I wanted. I was often far too transactional, and the surveys reflected that.

I've always been sarcastic—a trait that can be funny and elicit laughter but isn't always effective for teaching young adults. My early surveys were full of comments about my sarcasm. At the time, I thought I was doing a good job. My principal was happy, and parents weren't complaining. But the kids were right: My class could be better if I tempered the sardonic wit, and their feedback helped me improve much faster than I ever would have on my own.

Using Feedback to Become a Better Coach

When I became a head coach, I carried this same process into athletics. At the end of each season, I asked athletes to evaluate the team and coaching staff. The feedback I received on these surveys tended to be more critical than those in the classroom—sports naturally bring out more emotion. But I worked hard to focus on the substance of the feedback rather than my own emotional response to criticism.

Their feedback led to many changes in my coaching career. Was I acting like a tyrant? How did that impact the team? Did athletes dislike the workouts? Was that because the workouts were ineffective, or had I failed to explain the training process? Many of their comments led to changes, either in the process itself or in how I communicated our expectations and goals going forward. Thanks to this feedback, I grew quickly as both a teacher and a coach.

A few memorable comments from athletes and parents stuck with me over time, including the following:

"Mr. Emeott is a bully, he is only concerned with winning the argument and never listens to his students."

"Coach Emeott only cares about the stars on the team, if you do not score he does not care."

"Mr. Emeott is too sarcastic and not funny."

"I do not think Coach Emeott knows anything about distance running, he is just a pole vault coach who was forced to coach Cross Country."

"I do not think Coach Emeott even knows my son's name."

"The attendance policy is way too strict; Coach needs to understand Track is not that important."

The more honest, unbiased, and anonymous the feedback, the faster the learning curve. As a young coach, I believed workouts and training were the most important aspects of success. Over time, I realized that relationships and culture are what truly drive great teams.

Helping Coaches Grow Through Feedback

As an athletic director, I counsel young, inexperienced coaches about the learning curve. I make it clear that their first year will be their worst—no matter the team's level of success. It will be their least experienced year, full of mistakes, and the only way to improve is to learn from them.

I now require every team at East Kentwood to conduct athlete and parent surveys about their experience with the coaching staff. The survey is simple:

- Rate your coach on communication, team culture, and overall experience.
- What did you like about your coach?
- What could they improve?

This is an invaluable tool for promoting growth.

As an athletic director and coach who has won eight state titles, I have some credibility, and my feedback is generally well received. However, when a first-year coach sits down to review their evaluations, it can be overwhelming. Sometimes I give them the option to read the raw surveys themselves or let me summarize them; not everyone is ready for harsh criticism. Some need feedback delivered constructively.

A Lesson in Growth

A few years ago, I walked into a restaurant to meet a friend who was running late. While waiting, I ran into a former parent from my first year as a head coach. It was obvious he had been at the bar for a while, and with some liquid courage, he was ready to share his truth with me.

His son had been on my team during my first year, by far my worst year as a head coach. He wasted no time telling me, "You were a horrible coach and did nothing to help my kid." His son had earned a scholarship to a major Division 1 track school in the Southeastern

Conference. But the dad insisted that his son would have been better off at a different high school and that I had been a low point in his athletic career.

I knew he was looking for an argument, but I also knew the truth: He was probably right.

Compared to the coach I had become, I wasn't very good back then. I made a lot of mistakes. So, I did something unexpected: I apologized. The truth was, his son may have been extremely talented, but he was also a handful. He showed up late, was disrespectful to coaches and teammates, and frequently lied. But in my early years, I was too transactional: more focused on what an athlete could do for the team than their development as people.

If that same athlete were on my team today, he'd have two choices:

- Change and commit to our standards.
- Be removed from the team.

I could have served him better. Instead, I took the easy road and let him run fast while ignoring the bigger issue of his attitude.

Feedback is important, even the unpleasant remarks from a parent in a restaurant bar. Good, bad, or otherwise, feedback will quickly direct your improvement as a coach. The learning curve should be steep. A lack of feedback leads to stagnation, and athletes deserve better.

Athlete Profile: Trevor Stephenson, Class of 2018

Trevor Stephenson is the son of our girls' head coach and hurdle coach, Stephanie Stephenson. Before his freshman year, Stephanie asked if I'd be willing to take Trevor on as a pole vaulter. At the time, Trevor was primarily a hockey player—a goalie, to be exact. He was short, skinny, and didn't quite fit the mold of a typical track athlete. Stephanie just wanted him to have something to do during the spring season while she was coaching.

That goalie mindset carried over into his pole vaulting—quiet, unassuming, and incredibly cerebral. Trevor wasn't a natural, but he was hooked. He listened intently, absorbed every bit of instruction, and worked harder than most kids I'd ever coached. He wanted to get better.

By the end of his freshman year, Trevor had cleared nine feet. Not enough to earn a varsity letter, score points, or qualify for anything—but it was a start. As a sophomore, he grew a little, got stronger, and started showing real promise. He soaked up feedback like a sponge and improved fast. That year, he cleared 13'6"—a massive jump forward.

Coaching Trevor taught me something valuable. For some athletes, the tone of my voice didn't matter, only the words did. Trevor had played years of hockey, where getting yelled at was part of the game. He trained himself to tune out emotion and lock in on specific, actionable advice. A vague "just do better" meant nothing to him. He needed to hear, "Keep your trail leg long" or "Don't let your feet dip at takeoff." That pushed me to become a better coach—less emotional, more technical.

By junior year, Trevor cleared 15'3.5" at the New Balance Indoor Nationals and placed at the MHSAA state meet. His senior year started with him as the starting goalie on the hockey team, still trying to sneak in indoor track training. Then in January, he broke his collarbone playing hockey. For most athletes, that injury would've ended their track and field season. But Trevor didn't disappear—he studied. He became a student of the sport, analyzing video, watching film, asking questions. When he returned to vaulting in early March, it was like he hadn't missed a day.

That spring would become one of the greatest seasons in Michigan high school pole vault history. He cleared sixteen feet early in the season and set his sights on five meters (16'4.75") by season's end.

The MHSAA state finals were hosted on our home track at East Kentwood. Trevor had grown into his six-foot-two frame and was clearly the best vaulter in the state—at least in our minds. We expected him to win. But another vaulter, Eric Harris from Saline, had other plans.

What followed was the most epic pole vault competition I've ever witnessed.

Trevor was first in the order, Eric second. Both cleared every bar cleanly through sixteen feet on their first attempts—no misses. At 16"3", Trevor missed his first attempt. Eric made his.

In pole vaulting, tiebreakers matter. If two athletes clear the same height, the one with fewer misses is ahead. You don't gain anything by simply matching someone—you have to beat them at the next bar. This is called a "miss-pass" situation.

Now trailing, Trevor passed his remaining two attempts to 16'6.5", a new state meet record. He cleared it on his second attempt. Eric also made it on his second attempt, keeping the pressure on. They both advanced to 16'9.5". Because Eric had cleared 16'3" on his first try, he still held the lead. If no one made 16'9.5", Eric would win.

By this point, the stadium was electric. Hundreds of fans crowded around the pit, and every jump was met with a rhythmic clap that grew faster as the athlete charged down the runway. I have never been in a more intense sports environment before or since.

Trevor missed his first attempt at 16'9.5". The jump was decent but needed adjustment. In that moment, my job wasn't to celebrate or stress—it was to steady him. Between jumps, I reminded him: "Keep your speed up, jump tall at takeoff, don't let your feet dip." Pole vault is a true partnership between coach and athlete. Every adjustment matters.

On his second attempt, the crowd began its slow clap—clap . . . clap . . . clap-clap-clap—building as Trevor started down the runway. He planted, launched, and sailed over the bar. The place erupted. Trevor sprinted into my arms, and for a moment we were both over the moon. He had taken the lead, and we felt that bar would win the meet.

From there, the competition was essentially decided. Eric passed his last attempt to 17', but neither athlete cleared it. The moment Trevor soared over 16'9.5"—a new all-time state record—was the championship moment every coach and athlete dreams of. He was locked in, fueled by both the crowd and the technical focus we had rehearsed countless times.

It was one of my proudest moments as a coach, and I'll always be grateful I got to share it with such a great kid.

CHAPTER 21

Excellence Is the Standard

Excellence is not an act but a habit. We are what we repeatedly do.
—Aristotle

WHAT ARE YOUR standards? At Kentwood Public Schools, our motto is "excellence and equity." In our track program, excellence is the standard. Whether on the track, at home, or in the classroom, we hold ourselves accountable to this expectation. Have you ever heard the phrase "good enough"? For us, it never is. This philosophy guides everything we do.

In every classroom in America, each student begins the semester with the ability to earn an A. By definition, an A represents excellence. Think about it in those terms, reviewing the following grade scale we are all familiar with:

- A = Excellent
- B = Good
- C = Average

- D = Poor
- E/F = Failing

If everyone has the opportunity to achieve excellence, why would you ever settle for less? The classroom, unlike other areas of life, has no defensive side; it is not a zero-sum game. You can achieve an A without affecting the success of your classmates. Similarly, in track and field, there's no defense—if I break four minutes in the mile, so can everyone else in the race.

Encourage your athletes to approach the classroom with the same mindset. There's no limit to how many students can be excellent. Excellence is the standard—live up to it. I often ask a student struggling in class, "Tell me about the students who are getting A's. Are all of them smarter than you? Some may actually have God-given talents in the classroom, but not all of them. How are they playing the game better than you?"

Excellence in All Areas

Imagine you're looking for a new mechanic and ask me for a recommendation. My response carries weight. If I say, "My mechanic is excellent," your search ends there. If I say, "They're good," you might hesitate. If I say, "They're average," you'll likely keep looking.

Excellence sets the standard; everything else falls short.

Our program isn't just about being excellent on the track. It's about being an excellent student, son, daughter, sibling, or neighbor. Take a moment to reflect on the people in your life who are truly excellent. What sets them apart? The truth is, at the outset, most people are average by definition. Excellence requires effort, time, and commitment, and it's not achieved by accident—it's a deliberate process.

I have athletes who are amazing at video games. They have spent countless hours training, purchased the best equipment, and watched endless YouTube videos studying strategies and experts. Students often understand the process of greatness because it already plays a role in their interests and pursuits; it's all around them. Social media is filled with musicians, athletes, and entrepreneurs talking about their journeys, the years of work before they ever found success. As coaches, our job is to help athletes connect the dots between those lessons and their own potential.

Growth Toward Excellence

We also make sure to applaud growth, the foundation of excellence. If an athlete was a poor student as a freshman and worked hard to become an average student, that's still growth. We celebrate that. But we won't stop pushing them either, because excellence is still the goal.

Who are considered to be excellent coaches in your field? Who are the standout coaches locally or in your state? What are the similarities and differences between your coaching style and theirs? These questions are a great start to self-discovery.

Athlete Profile: Jon Henry, Class of 2010

Jon Henry was the third-string quarterback on the freshman football team when I first heard his name. He was a hardworking kid with great grades who didn't need much extra guidance. His mother was always present—an incredible parent—and his stepfather, though often behind the scenes, was a great role model who instilled a strong work ethic.

Overcoming Setbacks and Rising Through the Ranks

As a freshman, Jon had a solid year in track, even competing in a few varsity events. His sophomore year, however, brought a major setback. While squatting in the weight room, he tore his hamstring, separating it from the connecting bone. It was an injury that could have derailed his athletic career.

But Jon wasn't wired that way. In the offseason between his sophomore and junior years, he committed himself to workouts, doing whatever he could to improve. At the same time, he had moved up the ranks in football and was now the starting quarterback.

Jon was the epitome of "Excellence is the standard." I'm not sure how much natural talent he had, but I knew one thing: He was going to get everything out of himself. He was quiet, unassuming, and relentless. He worked hard every single day, driven by an undeniable desire to be great.

Breaking Through and Becoming a Champion

During his junior year, Jon started to come into his own as a sprinter. He was coached by our amazing sprint coach, Jeff McCune. Despite competing in many races, he hadn't yet actually won one. He had always been bested by either an opposing team's runner or his own teammate, Tyrone Green, a blazing-fast senior.

At the state meet, Jon looked incredible in the preliminary rounds, setting up a showdown between him and Tyrone in the 100-meter dash finals. That day, Jon finally won his first-ever race on the biggest stage: at the state meet at home. Not a bad race to win.

A few weeks later, we traveled to the national championship meet in Greensboro, North Carolina. We had a fairly uneventful showing, placing in only a few events, but the talent we competed against was on another level. On the way home, Jon turned to me and said, "How are we ever going to beat them? They are bigger, stronger, and faster!" I could tell then that this was not Jon being defeated. This was Jon legitimately wondering what it would take over the next year to overcome these seemingly super human athletes.

Jon had already turned the page. While others were satisfied, he was already thinking ahead to the 2010 national championships, determined that next time we wouldn't just show up. We would be able to compete with the best in the country.

Senior Year and the Tattoo

That summer, like many of my athletes, Jon decided to get a tattoo. Some of the guys went for large chest pieces with words like "blessed" or "flash." Jon, however, got a giant tattoo on his arm, which was clearly visible in all of our sleeveless track uniforms. Tattoos seemed to be the trend that year.

As an older coach, I didn't understand the fascination with tattoos. I often expressed my concerns, warning them they might regret these decisions in the future. It seemed to collide with their more conventional achievements: the straight-A student, the state champion sprinter, the kid who always did everything the right way—now with a lifelong, giant tattoo. Today, it doesn't seem like a big deal, but in 2010, tattoos were just starting to become socially accepted, and high school athletes were getting them more frequently.

The Perfect Season

Jon had a flawless senior season in track and field. At the state meet, he won the 100 meters, 200 meters, 4×100 relay, and 4×200 relay.

The following week, our 4×100 relay team competed against an all-star squad of the best sprinters from Ohio and Indiana—an EK-versus-everyone moment. We dominated, winning at 41.15 seconds and reclaiming our own state record.

A week later, we returned to the national championships. This was what Jon had been planning for all year. Jon had not forgotten that feeling of a year ago. Jon had witnessed greatness and he held our team to that standard all year, we were ready to compete on that level. And this time, we didn't just compete against the best teams in the country—we won. By the end of the weekend, our team was crowned national champions, an incredible feat for a Michigan school.

Beyond High School: A Scholar and an Athlete

After high school, Jon accepted a full-ride scholarship to play football at Western Michigan University. After his freshman year, Jon doubled down on the tattoo idea—this time, getting a front-facing neck tattoo, and not a small one either. It was bold and prominent for everyone to see.

As someone who had fought through many barriers in life, I couldn't help but comment that the tattoo might make things harder for him down the road. I even told him, "I'm not sure I'd trust a doctor with a neck tattoo to diagnose me with cancer." Jon just laughed. He wasn't worried about what people thought—he was focused only on what he could accomplish.

After a great career at WMU, Jon took full advantage of the opportunity and parlayed that free education into his next step: Harvard University.

He went on to earn a master's degree in biology from Harvard, using that degree as a launchpad for medical school. Today, Jon is still pursuing his dream of becoming a doctor—with a neck tattoo.

Jon at Nike Team Nationals in 2010

CHAPTER 22

Know Your Role: Parents

There are only two lasting bequests we can hope to give our children. One is roots, the other, wings.
—Hodding Carter

I T IS IMPORTANT that all participants understand their role in an athletic event. This responsibility goes beyond the athletes themselves and includes the adult leaders and mentors in various positions who support the athletes.

Coaches

As a coach, your job is to prepare your team to be in the best possible position by the time competition occurs. A good coach should have a general idea of how the contest will unfold before it even begins. The work leading up to game day—the training, strategy, and preparation—should leave nothing to chance.

A coach is also responsible for clear communication with athletes and parents regarding the details of the event:

- Who will compete?
- What plays will be called?
- What situations should the team expect?

Athletes

Athletes must focus on controlling the controllables. Leading up to competition, an athlete should take responsibility for factors that directly impact performance, including the following:

- Nutrition
- Sleep
- Mental preparation
- Attitude
- Effort in practice

Everything an athlete does leading up to game day influences their performance.

Athletic Directors

The athletic director hosts the event. This entails the following decisions and responsibilities:

- Start times and logistics
- Who is permitted in the game
- When doors open

- Access to teams
- Hiring officials
- Paying staff (ticket takers, event personnel, etc.)

Parents

The parents' role is simple: encouraging their athlete and the team, being positive, and remaining present. The child needs their parents the most when things don't go as planned. When athletes fail, they experience a lonely moment, one where they need their parents' support more than ever. Their job is to be there for them—not to fix everything, but to let them process the emotions of falling short.

As a parent, I have attended countless competitions, traveling long distances to watch my children and their teammates compete in both high school and college. My mindset has remained the same, with two things particularly emphasized:

- I am there to support when support is needed.
- I know I am needed most when my kids fail.

When my kids win, they are surrounded by friends and teammates celebrating. But when they lose? That's when the car ride home feels the longest. That's when I am needed most.

It is *not* a parent's role to do the following three things:

- Criticize officials
- Criticize other athletes
- Criticize coaches (especially during an event)

There are a time and place for discussing concerns with a coach, and it is never from the stands in the third quarter. I have never met a player who enjoys hearing their parents yelling from the stands. I have often wondered what drives this behavior when I witness it. Is it a learned response? Maybe one time, they yelled "Shoot!" and their kid took a shot and made a basket, unfortunately reinforcing the belief that their input was necessary.

From a coach's perspective, I have seen how this unfolds. Almost every time, the athlete is embarrassed. Too often, the parents' vocal comments from the stands contradict what the coach is saying. And even when a parent's advice is technically correct, the athlete is left in an impossible situation, with two conflicting options:

- Do they listen to the coach, the expert the school hired to lead the team?
- Or do they listen to their parent, the person who has raised, fed, and provided for them?

It's a lose-lose situation. Coaching an athlete is a bit like co-parenting, because it takes a village more than just two biological parents to raise a well-adjusted, successful child. When two voices are in direct conflict, the young athlete is caught in the middle, and that rarely ends well.

As competitors themselves, coaches do everything they can to improve their chances of winning. I have never seen a situation where an out-of-control, disruptive parent made an athlete play better. I have never seen a coach put a kid in the game or offer a scholarship because a parent pushed them into it by yelling from the stands. I have never seen a parent criticizing another athlete lead to more wins.

Most parents are passionate, and that's a good thing. But passion without purpose or control is a problem. Every parent has moments of feeling like their child should play more, that the coach made a bad decision, or that the refs blew a call. I have felt those things too. But I have also realized the following three things:

1. Everyone is doing their best, even if their best doesn't meet my standards.
2. If my child's current situation isn't good enough, there are options beyond acting like a fool in the heat of the moment.
3. If a coach is truly holding my child back from earning a full-ride scholarship, then I need to consider my options—a transfer, training differently, seeking additional coaching— but I need to do so with prudence and perspective.

The reality is that most kids aren't on the verge of a Division I scholarship, and the coach is probably less responsible for their future than you think.

In the same vein, it never helps to yell at an official. Coaches can sometimes work an official to get a call, but this is never helped by a parent's reaction. And criticizing another athlete? It is completely out of line for a parent to publicly berate someone else's child, and it almost always leads to unnecessary conflict in the stands.

A few years ago, college coaches started asking one question before recruiting an athlete: "How are the parents?" Without naming names, I've seen firsthand how much this matters. Early in the transfer portal era of college sports, I would casually mention to a college coach that a kid might benefit from "getting away from home" because their parents were overbearing and never satisfied. I didn't realize at the time how much weight those words carried: Coaches would immediately cool on that athlete, and the recruitment process would stop.

College coaches have had to make huge adjustments in the way they recruit. Club and AAU coaches have known this for years: You are recruiting the parents as much as you are recruiting the kid. If a player's parents are difficult, the chances of them transferring after a year or two are significantly higher. At the college level, coaches invest time and effort into freshmen and sophomores with the expectation of a payoff in their junior and senior years. If they believe an athlete's parents will constantly look for something "better," they are far less likely to offer a scholarship.

With the transfer portal and "name, image, and likeness" deals changing college sports, coaches are more concerned than ever about what parents will do when their kid isn't playing or is benched. One college coach told me that when they scout players, they also watch the stands to identify the parents. If they can't figure out who the parents are by the end of the game, that's a good thing—it means they aren't a distraction.

From time to time, coaches will need to step in and play the role of a parent. But I have yet to meet a parent who needed to take on the role of a coach in the third quarter.

Athlete Profile: Reece Emeott, Class of 2026

Reece is my youngest son, and as I write this, he is a eighteen-year-old in his senior year at East Kentwood. He is the two-time defending state champion in the pole vault and aspires to compete in college.

Serving a dual role as parent and coach in his athletic career has been one of the hardest things I've done, especially given that I've also been the athletic director during his entire high school career and Reece competes in football as well as track and field. Watching his games through this unique lens has been an adjustment.

As a freshman football player, his team lost all nine games—a brutal season for any competitor. I sat in the stands and heard every complaint, every frustrated comment about the refs, the coaches, and the players. At the start of the season, Reece wasn't playing much, even though, deep down, I believed my son was good enough to be on the field. The same way every parent feels. Every negative thought a parent could have also ran through my head. But I constantly had to remind myself: These are the best coaches our school has to offer. They have *forgotten* more about football than I will ever learn. I told myself over and over, "If my son is truly as good as I think he is, the coaches will see it. That's their job."

At home, we kept things simple. After every game, we told Reece, "It was so much fun watching you compete today." And if he ever asked for advice, we told him, "Work extra hard in practice and make it impossible for the coaches not to play you."

Beyond that, I had to trust the process.

I was incredibly proud of how he handled that season. He faced adversity and disappointment, and he grew from it. The team didn't win a single game, and that's tough for any parent who supports their kid to forget. But when I look back, I honestly don't remember a single moment from the field on game days that season. What I do remember is watching my son start to understand the commitment it would take to become great. By the end of the season, Reece would wind up starting both ways, having developed his skills to the point that his coaches needed him on the field. There were still times I wanted to step in and ask questions, but I knew that wasn't my role. As athletic director, I could have called the coach into my office and given my opinion. I could have sent a simple email and had an official banned from working our games. But that wasn't my role.

My job was to love my kid, hold him accountable, and help him grow.

Losing is hard. I hate losing. My son hates losing. That freshman season was a master class in dealing with failure—but we learned a lot. Imagine if I had undermined his loyalty to his coaches and teammates by criticizing them at every turn. Instead, we taught him to trust his coaches and focus on controlling what he could control.

If I had told Reece that his best friend stunk at football and should be benched, how would he feel when that same friend came over for dinner, knowing how I had disparaged him? If I had told him he deserved a starting role and his coach was an idiot, he could have lost faith in his coaches—not just in football, but in any sport he played.

We see this all the time: athletes who don't trust their coaches because they've been taught by parents to be skeptical of them. They've been told some coaches are okay, but ultimately, their parents always know best. I never wanted to mislead Reece that way. The best thing I could do as a parent was support the process and help my child bring full effort and a great attitude every day.

Reece flying high!

CHAPTER 23

The Greatest Victory I Have Ever Been a Part Of

*The meaning of life is to find your gift. The
purpose of life is to give it away.*
—Pablo Picasso

A S A COACH, I've been fortunate to experience incredible successes: countless track meet wins, undefeated seasons, eighteen consecutive regional titles, eight state championships, and even a national title. But when I look back, the greatest victory of my career didn't come with the biggest trophy or happen on the grandest stage. It happened in 2004, during my first season as head coach at East Kentwood, when a perfect storm of events created a moment I'll never forget.

A Season of Challenges

Before I came on board, East Kentwood had a proud tradition, but it wasn't exactly a dominant powerhouse in track and field. I was only the third coach in the program's history. First, there was Pat Patterson, who coached from 1968 to 1980. He passed away suddenly just about a month before the 1980 season, and his name graces our stadium. My mentor, Chuck Drnek, took over in 1980, and I worked under him for six years, beginning in 1998. Finally, it was my turn. When I took over in 2004, the team was solid, but not great. We were coming off years of strong league competition in the highly competitive OK Red conference, which had twenty-five conference titles from 1966 to 2003.

We had a few standout athletes but lacked depth. To make matters worse, the conference had just added Forest Hills Northern, the reigning Division 2 state champions, led by future All-American hurdler Josh Hembrough. We suffered a brutal loss to them in our first meet of the season. Our second loss came against Rockford, our biggest rival. That meet was closer, but it was still a loss. We became the first team in East Kentwood history to suffer two dual meet losses in the same year.

I was the losingest coach in school history. Back then, there was a chat board called Mlive Forum. This was an anonymous chat room and would have specific threads such as West Michigan Track and Field. There were many comments from alumni and parents about the new coach at EK and how he had tarnished this once dominant program. Obviously, this was not a fun time as a young coach.

Heading into the conference championship meet, we had two losses, Forest Hills Northern had one, and Rockford was undefeated. The only way we could salvage a championship season was to win the OK Red conference meet. And even that wouldn't be enough on its own—Forest

Hills Northern had to finish second, and Rockford third. It was the only way to create a three-way tie for the league championship.

Planning for the Perfect Storm

As a young coach, I spent countless hours analyzing the meet on paper. I poured over every detail, tweaking our lineup and predicting the moves of other teams. By meet day, I had crafted the perfect lineup. When I scored the meet predictively on paper, the result stunned me:

- Rockford: 110 points
- Forest Hills Northern: 112 points
- East Kentwood: 113 points

It was possible—but just barely.

I gathered the boys and told them, "There's a chance we could win this, but all the stars and moons must align at the same moment." Throughout the day, points were gained and lost in every event. Some athletes faltered, but others stepped up in ways we couldn't have anticipated.

Heading into the final event, the 4×400 relay, the score stood as follows:

- Rockford: 108.5 points
- Forest Hills Northern: 107 points
- East Kentwood: 106.5 points

The math was simple, demanding that we win the relay, Forest Hills Northern place second, and Rockford place third. Any other outcome, and our dream of salvaging the season and potentially my coaching career was over.

The Race of a Lifetime

The 4×400 relay is the greatest event in all of track and field, and this race did not disappoint. It is the final race at nearly every track meet in the world, the culmination of a day filled with competition. Each team brings together a group of four strong athletes—often from different event disciplines—each running one lap of the track.

Whether it is the closing event of the Olympics or the final race of a middle school dual meet, the 4×400 is almost always compelling. It showcases the heart, speed, and determination of a team's best competitors, often delivering the most emotional and dramatic moments of the day.

Our team was made up of our four best runners: Jeremiah Nelson, Bryan Lochan, Tony Phan, and our anchor, Ray Wilson. Ray was our best 800-meter runner that year. From the start, our lead-off leg, Jeremiah, got us out fast. By the first baton exchange, it was already clear that it would be a three-team race: East Kentwood, Forest Hills Northern, and Rockford had pulled far ahead of the rest of the field. While we needed a very specific outcome to win the championship, we couldn't control what other teams did—all we could do was run our race and fight for the victory ourselves.

At the second exchange, Forest Hills took the lead, with Rockford trailing just behind. Through the third leg, we gained ground on Forest Hills, but Rockford remained right there. As we approached the final exchange, the race was dead even: three teams, three incredible anchors, and everything on the line. We had our guy, Ray Wilson, with the stick and one lap to go. No one was a bigger EK fan than Ray, and he knew what this all meant for his team and his school.

One race. One lap. One moment to define a season.

Each anchor took turns leading at different moments in that final leg. You could feel the tension in the entire arena. And then—on the home stretch—Ray pulled away. Behind him, Forest Hills Northern edged out Rockford for second place.

The final scores were as follows:

- East Kentwood: 116.5 points
- Forest Hills Northern: 115 points
- Rockford: 114.5 points

We had done it—a three-way tie for the conference championship, the first title of my coaching career.

Relief, Not Just Joy

I was elated. The stress of the season had taken its toll—I had lost twenty-five pounds, mostly from stress and lack of eating. But at that moment, it felt like two hundred pounds had just been lifted from my shoulders.

We had salvaged a championship season that day, and it felt amazing. I was so proud of those kids. As the night wound down, I sat alone in the stands, watching our team take a shared victory lap with Forest Hills Northern. Rockford had already boarded the bus, missing what was truly a special moment.

My track and field throws coach—Hall of Fame football coach John Shillito—walked up to me with a big smile and said, "David, that will be the greatest victory of your life." At the time, I didn't understand. *What is he talking about?* I thought. *We're going to win so much more.* But he continued: "From now on, victories like this won't feel the same. You'll have expectations of success, not just hopes and dreams of it. From now on, a conference title will feel like relief—not pure joy."

John was right. I've celebrated many championships since that night, but none have ever felt quite as magical as that one. That night, walking across the moon-lit track toward our bus was one of the most calm moments I have ever experienced.

Athlete Profile: Alex Mirandette, Class of 2004

Alex Mirandette joined the team as the younger brother of state champion pole vaulter Erik Mirandette. At first, I encouraged Alex to explore other events, thinking that distance running might be a better fit and help him avoid the pressure of living in his brother's shadow. But Alex was determined to follow in Erik's footsteps.

As a freshman, Alex was the smaller, skinnier sibling who cheered loudly for his brother after finishing his own events. Over time, he worked hard and improved significantly. By his senior year, he had become a team leader, and his leadership set the tone for a particularly challenging season.

Alex led through relationships. He wasn't the type of leader who directed others; instead, he led by example and by the way he cared about those around him. When I think about that season, I remember being thrown into the role of head coach. I had to spend more time with the entire team and less time with the pole vaulters. In previous years, I had been solely focused on pole vaulting and would spend hours with that one group. Now, with sixteen other events to manage, the pole vaulters wouldn't get nearly as much of my attention as they were used to.

Alex stepped up and became an invaluable asset. He made sure the pole vault group continued to grow, and even beyond his years at EK, his influence as an effective pole vault team leader set the tone for every leader of that group since.

During his senior year, Alex found himself in the middle of a controversy when a fellow student spread some rumors about his relationship with his girlfriend. It was the kind of situation that can be a big deal to high school kids, often resulting in fights and division. When I asked Alex about it, he simply said, "If people know me, they know that's not true. If they choose to believe it, I'm okay with that too. My character will speak for itself." His handling of this hurtful gossip spoke to his precocious maturity and wisdom, qualities that also benefited his track and field leadership.

The theme of that season, led by guys like Alex, was to care about each other and fight for the team. They remained united as underdogs, never losing faith in one another. It was a season defined by powerful leadership and deep relationships, all led by Alex's example.

At the unforgettable conference championship meet, Alex not only won the pole vault, but his leadership played a key role in our team's victory. It remains the greatest win of my career, and Alex was at its heart.

After graduation, Alex moved to Spain and then Morocco with his brother to help rebuild homes that had been destroyed by an earthquake. His commitment to serving others was always his highest priority. Toward the end of their time abroad, Alex and his brother embarked on a final, 9,000 mile journey from South Africa to Egypt on dirt bikes with a close friend. On the eve of their return to the United States in 2005, nearly a year after graduation, they were the victims of a suicide bomber in Egypt. Erik survived with injuries, but tragically, Alex was killed by the attack in a Cairo marketplace.

His story is told in the book *The Only Road North,* by Erik Mirandette.[5] Alex had wisdom beyond his years, and his life was taken far too soon.

That experience changed me. It reminded me to appreciate the journey, because we never know how soon the road might end. My time with Alex was far too short, but I will always be grateful for the memories and the lessons he left behind. His presence continues to shape my career. He reinforced something I've always believed: Care

---

5   Erik Mirandette, *The Only Road North: 9,000 Miles of Dirt and Dreams* (Zondervan, 2007).

about kids every day, because they are more than athletes; they are people, and every moment matters.

To honor Alex's legacy, we renamed our Track Athlete of the Year award the Patterson/Mirandette Award and placed a memorial rock near the pole vault pit. My family's personal tribute was giving our youngest son, Reece, the middle name Alex.

Erik (middle), me (left) and Alex (right) celebrating Alex's
Pat Patterson Award. The award has been renamed
the Patterson/Mirandette Memorial Award.

CHAPTER 24

Building a Lasting Culture

Culture eats strategy for breakfast.
—Peter Drucker

O
VER A LONG career of coaching competitive teams, one of my proudest achievements is the consistency we've maintained. While we've had the occasional subpar season, we've mostly remained at or near the top, year after year. What fascinates me, though, is how fleeting success can be for many teams. Every few years, there seems to be a "hot new team," but many fade just as quickly as they appear. This phenomenon happens at both the state and national levels.

Why is sustained success so difficult? Schools' talent levels don't vary significantly year to year. Of course, once-in-a-lifetime athletes can tip the scales, but in team sports, where success depends on the collective, the real difference is culture. Have you built a culture of winning, or are you just winning because of a temporary influx of talent?

The Foundation of a Winning Culture

Coaching a track team is like coaching six teams at once—throwers, pole vaulters, sprinters, hurdlers, distance runners, and jumpers. Each group develops its own identity and culture within the team. Over the years, I've observed these "mini-cultures" evolve, sometimes thriving and sometimes struggling.

What's become clear is that a lasting culture depends on leaders who understand their impact not just for today but for tomorrow. A true leader doesn't just win; they leave a legacy.

As a transformational coach, it is important to discuss legacy when working with great teams. There are times when a team will have a banner year—winning a championship or moving from the bottom of the league to being a contender—only to return to last place the following season. Did the team not benefit from its time at the top? Did the message of hard work and commitment not reach the underclassmen?

When it comes to legacy, leaders need to recognize their immense responsibility. A true leader should be proud of what they leave behind. A selfish leader might leave behind trophies, but a group of true leaders will leave behind a future generation of champions.

I often challenge our athletes with this: What kind of culture will you leave behind? Will next year's team be better because of you? When you return to visit after college, will your old teammates be excited to see you, or will they have moved on as if you were never there?

As coaches, our job is to create and nurture leaders who set the tone for the team. These leaders inspire the next generation, keeping the team's standards high. What makes a lasting culture isn't just winning—it's how you win, including the traditions and values you leave for those who follow.

Embracing the Crazy

Every year, we emphasize the value of being "crazy" for your sport. The best athletes—the ones who truly separate themselves—are often wired a little differently. They're the ones doing extra reps when no one's watching, staying late after practice, or training in extreme conditions. Their stories of dedication become team legends. I am sure everyone reading has an athlete in mind right now who fits this bill.

When I first took over as coach, we had good athletes. Over time, we built something even more powerful: a culture that celebrated passion and work ethic. We tell stories of past athletes and the standards they set, not just for nostalgia's sake but as a blueprint for success. These legends inspire the current team, showing them what's possible and raising the bar for everyone.

We remind our athletes of those who came before them—the distance runner who finished as an NCAA runner-up, the pole vaulter who made the world team, the thrower who became a professional football player for the Dallas Cowboys. These stories aren't just about talent. They're about relentless work.

A Warning from COVID-19

The COVID-19 pandemic put our culture to the test in ways we couldn't have anticipated. In 2020, just three days into what could have been our greatest season ever, the world shut down. We had the top thrower, hurdler, and jumper in the state, along with an amazing group of seniors who had won three straight state titles. That year, we had planned to use the season to groom our underclassmen for leadership. But instead, the season was wiped out, leaving everyone devastated—including my own children, who were on the team.

The following year, COVID-19 restrictions made it nearly impossible to rebuild our culture. Daily meetings were reduced to less than six minutes outdoors with at least six feet between athletes. All of our culture talks were gone. By 2022, the lack of leadership and passion was glaring. We had relied on culture's unifying, natural ability to share information for so long that we had stopped teaching the basics. One day, at practice, I quizzed the team on simple track knowledge with the following questions:

- How many points do you score for winning an event?
- If you drop the baton, can you still finish the race?
- Can you purposely knock over hurdles?

The coaches and I were stunned. The kids knew almost nothing. Our leaders hadn't passed down the fundamentals because we didn't have leaders in place to do so. Our once-dominant culture had been wiped out.

Rebuilding a Culture

Building a culture of excellence isn't immediate—it takes time. When we first started coaching, it took five years to win our first state title, and I assumed now that rebuilding would take just as long. We needed new leaders who could connect with their teammates and inspire them to be great. And we, as coaches, needed to stop relying on talent and begin focusing on building connections and values again.

So, we got started. We took a step back and began to reflect on the decisions we were making. Were we truly living out the values we preached: consistency, effort, attitude, and dedication? Or had we started sacrificing transformational coaching for talent? Had we become transactional?

Every aspect of our team came under scrutiny, and that started with me. While head coach during COVID-19, I had undergone major role transitions. I went from being a schoolteacher to an athletic director, and that shift changed the way I interacted with athletes. Without realizing it, I had started to distance myself—not intentionally, but simply because of how my time was being spent.

As my responsibilities expanded, I had to rely more on my staff. I no longer had the capacity to be as hands-on as I once was. This forced us to rethink how we could build relationships and continue to hold everyone accountable. We couldn't rely on proximity alone to work like osmosis; we had to be more intentional. As a teacher, I would be in the halls and lunchroom each day, and a fair percentage of my athletes would be in either my class or one nearby. Casual encounters were common. Now, it became clear that the strength of our program would depend on more deliberately empowering all of our coaches, deepening individual connections, and reinforcing the standards that made us successful in the first place. The entire coaching staff would need to carry more of the burden.

As I write this book, we're still rebuilding. I continue to tell stories of past legends, but I also know we need new stories to inspire the next generation. Can we do it again? Time will tell. But one thing is certain: We won't stop working to create a culture that lasts.

Athlete Profile: Jon Manby, Class of 2007

When I think of lasting culture, I think of Jon Manby. Jon was the kind of athlete who seemed a little crazy, but in the best way. He wasn't the most naturally gifted runner, but his dedication was unmatched.

Jon had been a strong member of our middle school program, and we were excited to bring him into the high school cross-country team. When Jon joined the team, I was the head cross country and the head track and field coach. His freshman year was solid, but he didn't qualify for the state meet. As a sophomore, he made the state finals but fell short of earning All-State honors. That result stayed with him and fueled a deeper commitment.

His journey to greatness truly began in the winter of his sophomore year. Jon made a decision to run every day, no matter the weather. On one particularly brutal snowy day, with wind chills around minus-twenty-three degrees and six inches of snow on the ground, Jon ran twelve miles alone. He wore shorts and toughed it out. It probably wasn't the smartest choice, but it became part of his legend and showed a level of toughness few have matched.

We set one clear goal: Jon needed to run 15:59 at the MHSAA state finals to place in the top thirty and earn All-State honors. Based on data from the previous fifteen years, that time was almost always enough to qualify. Every workout, every split, and every coaching decision that season was designed to help him achieve that mark.

The night before the state meet, Jon was feeling under the weather. He had a cold, and his confidence wavered slightly. But on race day, he locked in mentally. He kept telling himself that he belonged and could compete with anyone out there.

Race day conditions at Michigan International Speedway were brutal. The first eight hundred meters went straight into a fifteen-mile-per-hour headwind. The next portion of the race was protected by trees, and Jon passed the two-mile mark still in the top ten. The final mile circled and returned to the exposed track surface with the wind once again hammering the runners. Jon pushed through and held his position. He crossed the finish line in eleventh place with a time of 15:57. That year, 16:08 was the final qualifying time for All-State, nine seconds slower than what we had been training for and one of the slowest qualifying times on record due to the extreme conditions.

Jon became the first All-State cross-country runner at East Kentwood in over twenty years. In the seasons that followed, many more runners earned that honor. It started with Jon, but it certainly didn't end there.

Jon's legend is still shared in our cross-country and track programs. Some say he almost lost his leg to frostbite. Others talk about the twenty-mile runs he completed while training. Whether every detail is accurate or not, the message remains the same. Jon believed in the process and showed what was possible when you commit fully to the work.

Before Jon, long runs were often seen as punishment. After his time on our team, ten- to twelve-mile runs became a badge of honor. His mindset and leadership helped transform the culture of our program. Many athletes adopted his standard and pushed themselves further than they thought possible.

Jon went on to run at Grand Valley State University and had a strong collegiate career. But his greatest legacy lives in the example he set at East Kentwood. Today, Jon teaches high school social studies and coaches cross-country in Idaho Falls, where he continues to inspire others just as he did here.

Jon looking focused

Author's Note

ONE YEAR AGO, I sat down to write a book. I wasn't sure where it was going, but my reason for writing it was clear. I felt that the end of my competitive coaching career, at least at East Kentwood, had arrived. We had just finished twenty-fourth at the state meet. In fact, the only points we scored were the ten earned by my son Reece, who won the pole vault, the first sophomore to do so in state history. It was by far our worst finish in over twenty years, and I felt like it was time to take a step back and reflect on my career.

Maybe I was a little depressed. Maybe I was searching for the glory days and hoping to relive all the great things we had done. But the reality was hard to ignore. We were not the team we once were.

Over the next four months, I wrote what would become the core of this book. As I drafted each chapter and interviewed former athletes, I found myself asking questions. Why did we stop reading through the team laws? When did we stop giving daily character speeches? The truth is, many of the things that had made our team great had quietly faded. As a coach, I had grown complacent. The lessons on character went from being a daily ritual to only occurring once or twice a week. We even experimented with weekly inspirational videos. They were good, but they just didn't hit in the same way.

I also reflected on some of the decisions we made around discipline and culture, especially in the years following the pandemic. While it's no excuse, nonetheless, in the wake of COVID-19, we were restricted to speeches under five minutes. It became harder to gather the team together. We were discouraged from high fives and even hugs. And gradually, many of our core practices disappeared. The results showed it.

As the writing process continued, I began working with this year's team. Slowly, we started to bring back the strategies you've read about in this book. A group of mostly underclassmen, a team we weren't so sure about, suddenly became a pretty good squad. We went undefeated during the regular season. We won the OK Red conference title. We won the regional championship. We won the MITCA team state title. And we entered the MHSAA state finals undefeated in every meet we had entered.

At the state meet, we finished in seventh place—a strong top-ten finish. And every single one of our point scorers is coming back next year.

I can't guarantee where we'll finish on the podium next season. But I can guarantee this: We will focus on culture and character development. Our goal will be to coach transformationally rather than transactionally. We will invest time in getting to know our athletes. We will help them chase their goals. And we will spend less time worrying about outcomes and more time committing to the process.

That is what this book has reminded me. And that is how I want to coach moving forward.

"Tradition never graduates." We say this a lot around EK track and field. There are many parts of you that will leave this program but the traditions you uphold will remain. I am proud of all the men and women our program has had the opportunity to be involved with over the years. I discussed a few in this book, but there are so many more that I could have shared with you. These athletes are the reason we do the little things right every day.

Thank you to each and every member of the EK family for all you have given to me personally and my family.

Our program's history reflects the hard work and dedication of everyone involved:

- 42-Time Conference Champs: 1966–2025
- 23-Time Regional Champs: 1970–2025
- 16-Time MITCA Team State Champs: 1999–2025
- 8-Time MHSAA State Champs: 2009–2019
- National Champs: 2010

We rarely lose, but the lessons in this book aim at where we need growth the most: character.

I hope you enjoyed this book. For me, it was truly a labor of love.

A proud Coach Emeott at Hayward Field in
Eugene, Oregon, preparing to compete

Acknowledgments

WRITING THIS BOOK has been a journey of reflection, humility, and deep gratitude.

To the student-athletes of East Kentwood, thank you. Your stories, your growth, and your resilience are the foundation of this book. Each athlete could truly be a book in and of itself. You were never just athletes to me; you were family. Every season brought new faces, and each spring gave me the honor of playing a small role in your development as people. I am proud to have highlighted a few of you in these pages, but every one of you has left a mark on my life.

To my coaching staff and partners at East Kentwood, thank you for walking beside me through victories, setbacks, and lessons learned. This work has never been mine alone.

To Coach Stephanie Stephenson, thank you for being much more than just a colleague. You have been my coaching partner, our hurdles coach, and, as I often joke, the sister I never asked for but always needed. Your strength, knowledge, and commitment have helped shape both our program and this book.

Thank you to the many coaches who have invested in our athletes over the years:

- **Jumps**: Matt Burton, Melvin Harris, Greg Hudkins
- **Sprints**: Jeff McCune, Kevin Winne, Tim Stencil, Aaron Gardner, Aaron Carter, Preston Pierson, Justin Michalowski, Erik Dudley
- **Throws**: John Makinen, Randy Smith, Norm Zylstra, Tyler Pettit, Austin Caster, Chad Reagh, Mike Keogan, Darrel Davis
- **Pole Vault**: Brian Bolton, Colton Emeott
- **Distance**: Tim Gumz, Ray Antel, Art Kraii, Val Thomasma

To Blaine Brumels, thank you for always standing in the fire with me.

To Coach Frank, your belief in me long before I earned it changed the course of my life. I carry that forward every day.

To my family, I owe you everything. My wife, Heather, has stood by my side as I gave countless hours to "other people's children." She rarely complained, always supported me, and somehow understood the joy coaching brought me. Her strength and love have held our family together.

To my children, thank you for sharing your dad with hundreds of other kids. Colton was a five-time All-State athlete, a member of three MHSAA state championship teams, and a leader on some of the greatest teams we ever put on the track. He continued his career at Nebraska and then Grand Valley State University, where he became a multi-time Great Lakes Intercollegiate Athletic Conference champion and national qualifier. Macey had a strong high school pole vault career and competed for the track team at Saginaw Valley State University. She is an amazing young woman, so driven and determined, and I could not be prouder. She has become my right hand in running pole vault camps, clinics, and the Grand Haven Beach Vault. Reece has already won two individual state titles in the pole vault as a sophomore and junior. He is an incredible student and an even better human being. We look forward to whatever journey he chooses next.

To my mom, life was not always easy, but we got through it together. Your strength is part of everything I do.

To my editor, Stephanie Rondeau, and the team at Streamline Books, thank you for helping me bring this vision to life. Writing a book never seemed possible, but your guidance made it real.

To the Kentwood Public Schools community, thank you for giving me the chance to grow. I arrived as a young man with so much to learn, and you welcomed me from day one. I hope I've made you proud.

Finally, to every young person who has ever felt like a long shot: This book is for you. Stay in the fight. You matter.

East Kentwood Track Team Laws

1. Make your team better.
2. Be early—"early" is on time. Tardiness is a sign of disrespect.
3. Attend all practices.
4. Listen to your parents.
5. Set goals, not limits.
6. Say, "I'm sorry, it will not happen again," and mean it.
7. It is nice to be great but great to be nice.
8. Respect everyone—fear no one.
9. Do not make excuses.
10. Use good manners, not bad language.
11. The greatest discipline is self-discipline.
12. Know everything about something; know something about everything.
13. Be loyal—stand by your friends, family, and team.
14. Always strive for A's in all classes.
15. Be honest.

16. Proper apparel for meets is red, black, or white and has an E and a K on it.
17. With time, hard work beats talent.
18. Don't let anyone say you can't accomplish your goals, including family, friends, and coaches.
19. Do not wear jewelry to practice or meets.
20. Shake hands with all competitors, before and after each competition.
21. Say please and thank you when talking to officials.
22. Don't deceive, cheat, or steal.
23. More is expected of sophomores than freshmen.
24. More is expected of juniors than sophomores.
25. More is expected of seniors than juniors.
26. More is expected of captains than seniors.
27. More is expected of coaches than captains.
28. With great power comes great responsibility.
29. Luck is what happens when preparation meets opportunity.
30. Bring extra clothes to all meets.
31. Don't stretch before practice or meets. (Stretching is to develop flexibility, not for injury prevention.)
32. Stretch after practice, after meets, or at night.
33. Build a good reputation.
34. Have a watch and use it.
35. Do not anticipate the starter pistol.
36. Confidence comes from competence, and competence is a choice.
37. Be the kind of person you want your son to be.
38. Always deal peacefully when approached by anger, insults, and disagreements.
39. Stay for the entire meet; there will be a TEAM meeting after the 4×400.
40. Sometimes the race is over before it begins.

41. If you do not know why your coaches asked you to do something, ask.
42. If you are in a relay, know your exchange zone.
43. Do not knock over hurdles on purpose.
44. Do your homework and do not blame athletics for your lack of preparation. Plan ahead so you do not get behind.
45. Do the little things right.
46. Maximize your ability.
47. Forgive others.
48. Be reliable—do what you say you'll do.
49. Do not litter. Pick up after yourself and your teammates.
50. Follow the golden rule: Treat others as you would have them treat you.
51. Bring a lock and know your combination.
52. The difference between what we do and what we are capable of would solve most of the world's problems.
53. Get eight hours of sleep each night; rest helps your muscles to recover.
54. Have goals and a plan to achieve them.
55. Know when to warm-up and what a proper warm-up is.
56. Don't be average.
57. Help people in need.
58. Be considerate of others.
59. Listen to really old coaches.
60. Fill your bank with dollars not pennies.
61. Winning is not the only thing, but compete like it is.
62. Know your priorities—i.e., God, family, school, **athletics**, job, girlfriend, haircut, prom . . .
63. Before attempting anything fast, you should be sweating.
64. Always think positive—you must believe it to see it to achieve it.
65. Sit-up straight.

66. Lean in.
67. Ask one question.
68. Nod your head.
69. Track the speaker.
70. If you are not getting better, you are getting worse.
71. Believe in your coaches, but more importantly, believe in yourself.
72. Run in your lane, not on or inside the lane lines; not doing so may cost you an All-American certificate.
73. Double-tie your shoes.
74. Never quit.
75. Don't take advantage of others.
76. Be accepting of differences.
77. You will not melt in the rain.
78. Bring $5–10 spending money for invites.
79. Hard work transfers positively to all aspects of life—athletic potential does not.
80. Make sure your spikes are sharp.
81. Fail to prepare, prepare to fail.
82. Whether you think you can or you think you can't, you're right.
83. You talk, you teach; you listen, you learn.
84. Do not leave expensive things unguarded and unattended to.
85. In order to run with the big dogs, you must train with them.
86. Pride is your greatest training partner.
87. Dreams come true every day. What are yours?
88. Making mistakes is a part of life; lying about it does not have to be.
89. On meet day, stay out of the sun.
90. Turn in your uniform when your season is over.
91. Surround yourself with people you respect; avoid people you do not.
92. A handshake is a window into your character.

93. Be smart when you talk to the newspaper; they **_will_** print what you say.
94. Do the right thing all the time.
95. You must ride the bus to a meet unless you have been cleared by the AD's office.
96. It is not the size of the dog in the fight. It is the size of the fight in the dog (or falcon).
97. Never look back during a race.
98. Play by the rules.
99. Consider the consequences of your actions.
100. Know the difference between a want and a goal.
101. Keep your friends close and your enemies closer.
102. Get a good night's sleep two nights before a contest.
103. Eat healthy every day.
104. If your lane sticker falls off do not turn around and pick it up.
105. Tell your coach if you are hurt and see Mr. Chapel ASAP.
106. If you aren't nervous, then you aren't normal.
107. Never wear boxers when you run; your parents want grandchildren.
108. Save talking to the girls until after the meet.
109. Always bring toilet paper to big meets.
110. The greatest waste in the world is the difference between what we are and what we could become.
111. Have a plan even if you don't use it.
112. Make sure your uniform is legal.
113. Strive to do great things.
114. If you show me a person's ten closest friends, I will show you him. Pick ten good ones.
115. The only disability in life is a bad attitude.
116. Always turn around after the race to look for your teammates.
117. When your coach says it . . . do it—ask why later.
118. Read *Mind Gym* by Gary Mack; it will help you to deal with athletic pressure.

119. Greatness has never happened accidentally; *choose* greatness.
120. Don't talk when the coaches talk.
121. Do not run under the hurdles during a hurdle race.
122. Know what place you are in during field events. Be prepared for a jump off in the vertical jumps.
123. Be sure Coach always has updated info, i.e., email, home phone, cell phone, etc.
124. Know the important marks for your event, varsity letter, conference, and regional and state qualifier.
125. If you want to run track in college, make sure Coach Emeott knows.
126. Though no one can go back and make a new beginning, everyone can create a new ending.
127. If you are on a relay, all uniforms must match.
128. Have an email address; make sure it is appropriate to send to college coaches.

Any questions, comments, criticisms, and/or witticisms at this point in time?

Athlete Contract

Name _____

This contract will be agreed upon by all parties and followed through. The consequences of not following through on this contract may result in removal from the team.

1. Grades
   a. Must be on schedule to graduate
   b. Must pass all classes this semester
2. Respect
   a. Athletes will respect ALL coaches, all the time.
      i. No back talk
      ii. No nonverbal signs of disrespect such as eye rolls or sighing
      iii. Adhering to all reasonable requests
      iv. Including event selection
   b. Be respectful of all teammates.

3. Leadership
   a. All athletes are leaders; each action you make will impact your team around you.
   b. Lead by example.
   c. Younger, less experienced athletes are always watching; what will they learn?
   d. What habits will others follow?
4. Training
   a. Athletes will finish all workouts from beginning to end in the way they were designed.
   b. Athletes will trust the process.
   c. Athletes will be open and honest about all situations, injuries, concerns, and goals.
   d. If an athlete fails to finish a workout for any reason, there will be consequences.
   e. This includes:
      i. Quitting
      ii. Being asked to leave
   f. If an athlete is injured and cannot finish the workout, said athlete will take, at a minimum, one week off to heal and rest.
   g. Consequences of failing to train properly:
      i. Minimum of one meet suspension
      ii. Removal from the team
   h. Athletes will train with the EK team. All external workouts will be approved by EK staff. This will start on March 13 and end on June 15.

If, at any time, the coaching staff feels that you are a detriment to the program, you will be dismissed from the team.

Name two competitive goals you would like the team to help you accomplish:

1. _____

_____

2. _____

_____

Name two behavioral goals you will work on to be a better teammate:

1. _____

_____

2. _____

_____

Step 1. Sign and follow contract.

Step 2. Address the team. Apologize for behavior that is not becoming of a leader. Promise teammates you will try to be a better influence on everyone. Promise teammates you will lead by example. Explain to teammates that you understand you are on two strikes and you will be on your very best behavior.

Step 3. Address your coaches, apologize for past indiscretions, and explain that you are working to be a better teammate and athlete.

Athlete Signature _____

Parent Signature _____

Coaches Signature _____

Connect with the Author

Have questions, comments, criticisms, and/or witisms at this point in time?

I'd love to hear from you.

Follow & Connect:

Instagram: @david_emeott_author
Facebook: Dave Emeott – Coach and Author
Website: beyond-the-finishline.squarespace.com

Interested in hosting Dave for a keynote, podcast, or coaching clinic?

Visit the website or reach out through social media to discuss scheduling and availability.

If *Beyond the Finish Line* resonated with you, please consider leaving a review or sharing it with another coach, parent, or athlete who might benefit.

Keep leading and keep growing — even beyond the finish line.